LIBERATING JONAH

LIBERATING JONAH

Forming an Ethics of Reconciliation

Miguel A. De La Torre

ORBIS BOOKS

Maryknoll, New York 10545

Founded in 1970, Orbis Books endeavors to publish works that enlighten the mind, nourish the spirit, and challenge the conscience. The publishing arm of the Maryknoll Fathers and Brothers, Orbis seeks to explore the global dimensions of the Christian faith and mission, to invite dialogue with diverse cultures and religious traditions, and to serve the cause of reconciliation and peace. The books published reflect the views of their authors and do not represent the official position of the Maryknoll Society. To learn more about Maryknoll and Orbis Books, please visit our website at www.maryknoll.org.

Library of Congress Cataloging-in-Publication Data

De La Torre, Miguel A.
    Liberating Jonah : forming an ethics of reconciliation / Miguel A. De La Torre.
        p. cm.
    Includes bibliographical references and index.
    ISBN-13: 978-1-57075-743-3
    1. Bible. O.T. Jonah—Criticism, interpretation, etc.
2. Reconciliation—Religious aspects—Christianity. 3. Church and minorities. 4. Social integration—Religious aspects—Christianity.
5. Marginality, Social—Religious aspects—Christianity.
6. Multiculturalism—Religious aspects—Christianity. I. Title.
BS1605.6.R35D4 2007
224'.9206—dc22
                                        2007016443

For my colleagues and students at
The Iliff School of Theology

Contents

Preface

W<small>HO HASN'T HEARD</small> of the mythological story of one of God's prophets being swallowed by a whale? Maybe because the story seems like a fairy tale, it is dismissed as some type of children's fable. Frankly, I too paid little attention to the Book of Jonah. Then one day, a hallway conversation with a Euroamerican colleague who specializes in the Hebrew Bible led me to reflect more deeply on the message of this biblical book. He asked me if any writings existed on the Jonah story from the perspective of people from the margins of society. I could not think of any immediately. An initial search for commentaries on Jonah from disenfranchised perspectives left me empty-handed. Hence began my serious exploration and contemplation of Jonah. My initial consideration of this biblical book led me to conclude that Jonah was written by someone who was living on the margins of empire, proclaiming that God's mercies extend even to the oppressors. Hence the genesis of the book you hold in your hands.

What I found most compelling about the Jonah story is the theme of reconciliation. All too often, discussions about reconciliation originate with the group that the present culture happens to benefit—what can *we* do?—and the discussion is manipulated so as to continue benefiting the privileged. Rather than becoming a process that could lead to a new creation based on justice, the discourse on reconciliation is often reduced to how those with power and privilege within the social structures can reconcile with those who are marginalized, and to how harmonious co-existence can be created while preserving the power of the dominant culture.

In the United States, reconciliation from the perspective of the privileged becomes an exercise on how to establish a "pseudo peace," a peace that doesn't disturb white supremacy and class domination. But what would happen if any discourse on reconciliation began instead at the margins of society? How would reconciliation look if it were initiated from the underside of U.S. power and privilege?

The purpose of this book is to study the text of Jonah to find biblically based paradigms for developing forms of discourse *and* action that can lead to reconciliation between different races and socioeconomic classes within the United States. This country is increasingly a nation of diversity—of ethnic backgrounds, of rich and poor, of languages, and of religious beliefs. How can we construct models that foster reconciliation for our diverse and often disjointed community?

I will contend that Jonah is the story of the marginalized called by God to bring the "good news" of God's grace to an oppressive empire. Rather than joyfully undertaking God's commission, Jonah grudgingly evangelizes his oppressors, disappointed that God forgives those responsible for subjugating and eventually decimating the Jewish nation. The Book of Jonah serves as a model for how the marginalized within the dominant Eurocentric U.S. culture *should not* approach the concept of reconciliation. Although much can be gleaned from other faith traditions, this book will focus specifically on how marginalized Christian groups seek reconciliation from within their faith communities.

In an earlier book, *Doing Christian Ethics from the Margins* (Orbis Books, 2004), I argued that one of the major concerns of those who exist on the margins of society about the ethical discourse of Eurocentric academics is their typical lack of emphasis on praxis that can lead toward the liberation of the disenfranchised. In short, this is the failure of *doing* ethics. It matters little if these ethicists are conservative or liberal; they usually find common ground in how they conduct their ethical analysis. More notable is their failure to address in deeds, more so than in words, the constant inhumanity faced by the marginalized of society right now. This goes beyond individual piety or virtues, which fail to guide moral agents on how to act. I argue that any ethical deliberation that fails to make the reality faced by the least among us the point of origin cannot be called Christian, and any discourse that does not move from the abstract to actual praxis is certainly not Christian ethics.

If ethics is the path to liberation/salvation, and specifically where reconciliation can occur with the God of life, then any methodology used to assist the faith community in developing ethical programs must start with the experience of those most affected by the sin of oppression, and it must end by transforming such structures into a more just social order. In the quest for reconciliation, liberation, and salvation, I make use of the "hermeneutical circle" introduced in *Doing Christian Ethics from the Margins* (see the diagram on p. 8 below).

In the first chapter, "Reading the Story of Jonah," I tell the story of the original text while revisioning the story to provide a new way of seeing that which has become all too familiar. I do not intend to prove or disprove the historical accuracy of the biblical story. Rather, I will employ what feminist biblical scholar Elisabeth Schüssler Fiorenza calls a "hermeneutics of creative imagination." This is a process used to uncover those aspects of a story that are masked by the "standard" reading of a text, usually a reading that imposes on a text a theological view that tends to normalize and legitimize the power and privilege of a dominant culture. Such a reading of Jonah has ignored the power structures that historically existed within the Jonah narrative, reducing its message to a simple call for "believers" to evangelize "pagans." *Retelling* the familiar story of Jonah allows us to move from an ancient text to examine the present social location of the disenfranchised and to question present-day power structures.

The second chapter, "Who Was Jonah? What Was Nineveh?" provides a way to explore how certain social structures are constructed to marginalize the many and thus privilege a few. Who was Jonah and what does he represent? Who were the Ninevites? Who are the Ninevites today? What does it mean to be of the empire? How does one learn to be part of the empire? How do today's modern-day Ninevites amass power? How do they religiously justify their power and privilege? By asking these questions, the chapter attempts to raise consciousness of the causes for oppression and to unmask them. This use of social analysis helps us gain a deeper understanding of the reality of our world today. The "standard" reading of the Book of Jonah is shown to be from a dominant culture's perspective, a call to go to the heathen nations to proclaim God's message; if, on the other hand, the United States represents Nineveh and Jonah comes from the margins, the message is quite different. Jonah's responsibility is to hold the "empire" accountable to the principles of justice. If this is the case, then it is not those residing in the United States who are charged with going into the world to convert the pagans to God. Rather, the people who suffer in the shadows of the U.S. empire, whether within or without, are called to bring a message of salvation to the center of power and privilege.

The third chapter, "Reflecting on Jonah," attempts to ground ethics in reality. Failure to do so only makes concepts of justice and reconciliation too abstract for those who are dealing with the daily struggle of survival. Working multiple jobs to barely provide for one's family makes justice-based praxis an unaffordable luxury of time. Additionally, some from the margins, like Jonah, refuse to reach out to their oppressors because they want God to punish the oppressors for the suffering they inflict upon the marginalized. After all, Jonah is a grudging evangelizer of his oppressors; this wasn't his first choice. He is disappointed that his "unjust" God forgives those responsible for subjugating the Jewish nation. It is usually easier to run away from God's calling than to challenge those who use their power to keep the marginalized at the margins.

The fourth chapter, "Praying through Jonah," will provide the reader with a way to consider how reconciliation can be conducted or achieved. By "prayer" I don't mean locking oneself in a closet for a private conversation with God to gain wisdom and guidance. Instead, prayer is understood as a communal activity, the bringing together of the different members of the spiritual body to pray as one and struggle through the biblical text together. This prevents the doing of Christian ethics from being reduced to an individual pursuit; it must always be a communal activity.

"Pitfalls Jonah Should Avoid," the fifth chapter, examines possible obstacles that can short-circuit the process of reconciliation before it even gets started. The chapter will explore some of the structural reasons why reconciliation appears so elusive and why the entire venture appears hopeless. Why do those with power hesitate to move toward reconciling? What would it cost the privileged to establish justice? The chapter will also explore barriers that prevent the marginalized from reaching a state of reconciliation. A hermeneutics of suspicion will be employed to uncover how some marginalized groups can be complicit with present oppressive social structures, while others seek salvation in terms of liberation for their own group, damning the dominant culture to God's "justice."

The final chapter, "Case Studies: What Would Jonah Do?" examines possibilities for praxis that can lead to reconciliation. To deliberate solely on ethical *theories* of reconciliation is worthless if the theories are not directly implemented through praxis. This is not to dispense with ethical theory, but rather to recognize that for the disenfranchised, theory must be subordinated to praxis. I hope that this exploration of several case studies will provide readers with opportunities to derive their own ideas on how to do the work of reconciliation.

This book is possible because many have accompanied me on my own journey to Nineveh, the empire. I am grateful to the students in a class I taught at my previous institution titled "Toward Christian Reconciliation." I am indebted to Ben Sanders and Abbi Halfman who participated in this class and continued for a semester as my research assistants. I am also thankful to Susan Perry, who, once again, has served as my editor. As always, her fingerprints can be found on my work owing to her constantly prodding me toward more rigorous scholarship through the questions and suggestions she makes after reading the first drafts of the manuscript. Also, I wish to thank my office assistant, Debbie McLaren, who proofread this manuscript. Finally, I continue to thank my God for my family, whose patience and love provide the emotional support so desperately needed in order for me to do my scholarship.

Introduction

JONAH IS AN ASPARAGUS—at least according to the popular 2002 Christian film *Jonah: A VeggieTales Movie*. Moviegoers were introduced to a Jonah who proclaimed God's word: specifically, "to play nice, do good, and to wash their hands." However, when God told Jonah the asparagus to go to the city of Nineveh, a dirty city characterized by vegetables that slap each other across the face with raw fish, Jonah ran in the opposite direction. He wanted nothing to do with a people that participated in such filthy habits. Although Jonah wanted to see them pulverized, the prophet Jonah, along with moviegoers, learned the important message of the story of Jonah: God gives second chances.

With presentations like this, is it any wonder that many consider Jonah to be some type of fairy tale? After all, wasn't Pinocchio also swallowed by a whale? Reducing Jonah to a child's story that emphasizes the whale incident does a disservice to the rich message found in this biblical text, a message especially relevant to those on the margins of the dominant culture. Yet, surprisingly, few religious scholars of color have spent much time considering the text of Jonah. For me, the text provides insight into a question with which the oppressed of the earth must wrestle, lest they end up being as spiritually deaf as their oppressors. Like Jonah, they must ask: How can we relate to those who bring subjugation, misery, and death to our people, our loved ones, and ourselves? Jonah's response was to seek revenge through what ethicists call retributive justice, the approach of "an eye for an eye." Jonah, along with many others, failed to recognize the important biblical message of God's challenging call for reconciliation. This call may be as distasteful to people today, especially the marginalized, as it was to the prophet Jonah.

God's call to Jonah was God's call to the Israelites. But how could they reconcile with the Assyrians who had marginalized and disenfranchised them? The social, political, and economic structures created by the Assyrians brought death-causing events down on the Israelites.

How could this ever be made right? Could the Jewish mother who witnessed her son sadistically tortured by the Assyrian armies offer forgiveness, even if the Assyrians did not ask for it? Could the hungry Jewish girl who turned to prostitution because she was orphaned by the Assyrian invasion break bread in peace with those responsible? Could the living offer redemption in the name of their ancestors who died in slavery building up the Assyrian empire?

Can the consequences of oppression ever be remedied? After all, how can the marginalized come together with those who see no need, or have little desire for reconciliation? What motivation exists for those with privilege to create a more just situation, a situation that would require forsaking their power? In short, what does reconciliation require and whose initiative is it? God has made a preferential option for those who are marginalized and oppressed. What responsibility might they in turn have? Is God asking something of them, as God asked something of Jonah?

At the beginning, it is crucial to define "reconciliation" and to determine *who* should do the defining. It is important to recognize that those who benefit from the present power structures cannot be relied upon to define reconciliation, or to determine how to go about achieving it. Embedded within the social structures that have endowed them with power and privilege at the expense of the marginalized, those "at the top" cannot remain neutral about the nature of domination and oppression. Because their social location legitimizes unjust social structures as normative, members of the dominant culture are usually unable to be objective about the reality of their privileged positions.

Reconciliation is not difficult to define in a general way. Reconciliation usually connotes congruency or harmony. It is often used in managing personal finances: "I need to reconcile my bank statement." Reconciliation in this sense is understood as the process of checking one financial account against another to ensure accuracy. The term is also used in connection with interpersonal conflicts; for example, "My wife and I are attempting reconciliation by seeing a marriage counselor." In either case, reconciliation is understood as restoring harmony to a situation that is disjointed or in conflict.

But how can we restore congruency to a situation that never, at least in our lifetimes, experienced harmony? In such a case, reconciliation defined solely as an act of restoring a lost quality is insufficient. Rather than a process of restoration, reconciliation must be understood as a process of arriving at a new state of being, one perhaps that neither party has ever experienced. As a human process, reconciliation is then focused on becoming something new instead of achieving a congenial environment. And this new state of being through reconciliation can be called salvation.

When the Pharisees sought to trap Jesus by asking him to name the greatest commandment of the Law for humans, Jesus responded: "You shall love the Lord your God with all your heart, your soul, and your mind. This is the first and great commandment; the second is like it: you shall love your neighbor as yourself. In these two commandments all the Laws and the Prophets hang" (Matt. 22:37-40).[1] Jesus made it clear that these two commandments are interconnected and cannot be separated. To be faithful to one, requires obedience to both. Simply stated, one cannot love God while hating one's neighbor. As the first letter of John reminds us, "Anyone stating to be in the light, yet hating [another] is still in darkness. The one loving [the other] rests in the light, and no offense is in them" (1 John 2:9-10).

If salvation is manifested as love for both our God and our neighbor, and if a tree is known by its fruits, then those who dominate or oppress others—in the United States most often members of the dominant Eurocentric culture—are falling short because they do not love their neighbors (specifically their neighbors of color or a lower socioeconomic class) as themselves. Domination by members of a Euroamerican culture has created a history marked by the genocide of Native Americans, the enslavement of Africans, and dispossession of Hispanics throughout the Western Hemisphere. And this history thrives today in a

---

[1] Unless otherwise cited, all biblical passages are translated by the author from the original Hebrew and/or Greek.

global political strategy that continues to ensure the economic privilege of the empire of one nation at the expense of the two-thirds world[2] nations whose raw material and cheap labor are exploited for capital gain.

The theological perspective that arises from concerns about the marginalized and dispossessed has commonly been known as *liberation theology*. Gustavo Gutiérrez, considered among the first to shape intellectually the liberationist discourse, articulated its main themes as the following:

1. freedom from oppressive economics, political, and social conditions that force individuals to live in conditions contrary to the will of God;
2. freedom for individuals to take control of their destiny when facing every possible kind of servitude imposed; and
3. emancipation from both institutional and personal sin that breaks relationships with both God and neighbor.

In the deepest sense, grounded in stories of the exodus from Egypt and the story of the resurrection of Jesus Christ, liberation is salvation. Salvation ceases to be something that is otherworldly. This present life is not some sort of test of the future. Instead, salvation embraces every aspect of humanity, transforming it to its fullness in Christ (Gutiérrez 1988, xxxviii, 151). To be saved is to be liberated. If salvation is understood as the giving of new life (John 10:10), a *temporal life* that is abundant as well as an *everlasting life*, then it occurs when individuals are liberated from whatever prevents them from receiving life at its fullest. To a certain degree, the terms "salvation" and "liberation" have been used interchangeably by liberation theologians.

But how do we achieve salvation? How do we arrive at liberation? I maintain that reconciliation is absolutely key. To be saved or liberated is to be reconciled, both with God and with one's neighbor. If we define salvation as reconciliation with God and

---

[2] "Two-thirds world" is a term being used by those who come from what the dominant culture normally calls "the third world." Moving away from the hierarchical connotation implied in the term "third world," I prefer instead "two-thirds world" as a more accurate description of two-thirds of the land masses, resources, and humanity in today's world.

one's neighbor, then salvation can occur only if reconciliation has taken place. Estrangement among neighbors becomes a collective "unpardonable" sin, for separation from neighbors brings about separation from God.

Still, any quest for reconciliation cannot advocate premature peace. A desire to "forgive and forget" can bring about only a cheap reconciliation that sacrifices justice for the sake of serenity. Any refusal to dismantle the very structures responsible for oppression allows those with power and privilege to avoid addressing the causes of oppression. Nor can reconciliation be reduced to a bargaining process between adversaries learning to accept and live under repressive systems. Reconciliation is not a political strategy but a process of spiritual healing. It must end human bondage and it must heal rather than suppress unresolved pain. It must lead to justice, not substitute for it.

Reconciliation must have a spiritual dimension as reconciliation seeks to reconcile humans with their God and with each other, an essential concept of the gospel. Without reconciliation, the good news of Jesus Christ loses its reason and purpose. Christian churches throughout the United States preach salvation from their pulpits but often remain sadly complicit with the overall social and political structures of the land that sustain ethnic, racial, and class divisions. Churches that represent the values of the dominant culture all too often fail as agents of peacemaking and reconciliation, as is witnessed by their complicity with and/or silence about the violence visited upon historically marginalized communities in the United States.

It is also crucial to know *who* is seeking reconciliation. While a great deal has been written about *individual* repentance, forgiveness, and reconciliation, this book will instead focus on *group* repentance, forgiveness, and reconciliation. Some geographic locations that come to mind are South Africa during its journey away from apartheid;[3] Cuba and its conflicted relationship with the Miami Cuban-American community, and by extension the

---

[3] Russell Daye, *Political Forgiveness: Lessons from South Africa* (Maryknoll, N.Y.: Orbis Books, 2004); John W. De Gruchy, *Reconciliation: Restoring Justice* (Minneapolis: Fortress Press, 2002).

United States;[4] conflicts between Protestants and Catholics in northern Ireland; and the ethnic conflicts resulting from warfare in the Balkans after the collapse of the former Yugoslavia.[5] While the discourse of reconciliation is typically applied to communities enduring violent conflict, we should not forget that the quest for reconciliation is pertinent to all communities, including those communities that may appear to be peaceful but nevertheless contain alienated groups of people who have historically been denied justice. While much fine work has been done, and should continue, on ending violent conflict in other areas of the world, the focus of this book is on racial, ethnic, and class conflicts in the United States—specifically, between Euroamericans and the historically disenfranchised groups of African Americans, Asian Americans, Hispanics, and Native Americans.

Sadly, when racial, ethnic, and class reconciliation in this country is examined, it is usually done from the perspective of those privileged by the present power structures. Virtually every Christian faith tradition in the United States has issued some repudiation of its racist past, asking for forgiveness and encouraging some sort of reconciliation. Yet, as Martin Luther King Jr. observed some fifty years ago, the Sunday morning worship hour is still the most segregated hour in America. Why? Because the question is usually formulated as "What must *we* (who benefit from the present structure) do" as a Christian duty or obligation for those who are "beneath" us, those who are at the margins of our power and privilege?

When this type of question is asked, reconciliation becomes charity, pity, or paternalism, and justice becomes political correctness. Why have the antiracist initiatives of U.S. churches been powerless in bringing about any real progress toward reconciliation? This is not a difficult question to answer because historically no group holding power has willingly forfeited its privileged

---

[4] Miguel A. De La Torre, La Lucha *for Cuba: Religion and Politics on the Streets of Miami* (Berkeley: University of California Press, 2003).

[5] Miroslav Volf, *Exclusion & Embrace: A Theological Exploration of Identity, Otherness, and Reconciliation* (Nashville: Abingdon Press, 1996).

space for the good of the marginalized. Liberation is always demanded but seldom given.

What must "we" do for "them" places all hope the disenfranchised might have for justice on the actions of those who are most likely to suffer a loss of power and privilege if real and substantive progress toward reconciliation is made. This book will wrestle with two crucial questions. First, if those who benefit from the prevailing social structures refuse to repent, to yield their privilege, or at least some of it, and ignore that a need for justice exists, what hope do those who are marginalized have? And, second, how do the marginalized seek reconciliation with those who are privileged, those who prefer a social structure that assures their power within society?

Because of a lack of willingness to give up power, any hope for reconciliation must rest with those living on the underside of society. These are the people who yearn for justice. Their struggle for justice in a nation dominated by race and class oppression becomes the primary context for initiating any discussion of reconciliation. I maintain that the disenfranchised can define and forge a reconciliation that can lead to their own liberation and salvation, as well as the salvation and liberation of those who benefit from the present structures of domination. And what role then will members of the dominant culture play? They can accompany the marginalized in their struggle toward reconciliation and justice. Instead of paternalistically leading those who are "less fortunate" toward a reconciliation that is nonthreatening for those in power, they are to stand in solidarity with the oppressed, even at the cost of their own power and privilege.

To liberate Jonah becomes a process for U.S. marginalized communities to seek and find their salvation, and that of their oppressors, through a reconciliation to be worked out in "fear and trembling." Jonah becomes a possible model for disenfranchised communities who are committed to the work of justice. Consequently, the biblical story of Jonah becomes more than a children's fairy tale. Instead, it becomes a key text for marginalized communities who want to bring about change and move toward reconciliation. For this reason we now turn to the biblical story, to read it with new eyes.

THE HERMENEUTICAL CIRCLE FOR ETHICS

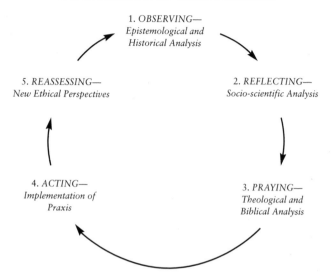

1. OBSERVING—
*Epistemological and
Historical Analysis*

5. REASSESSING—
New Ethical Perspectives

2. REFLECTING—
Socio-scientific Analysis

4. ACTING—
*Implementation of
Praxis*

3. PRAYING—
*Theological and
Biblical Analysis*

1

Reading the Story of Jonah

ONCE UPON A TIME, around the eighth century before the Common Era, the word of YHWH came to Jonah ben Amittai. This is neither the first time nor the last that YHWH's word has been revealed to humans. In fact, Jonah's call to proclaim the word of the Lord is reminiscent of how YHWH summoned other prophets, such as Elijah (1 Kgs. 21:17, 21), Isaiah (Isa. 38:1), and Jeremiah (Jer. 1:14; 11:2).

Jonah was from the land of Gath-hepher, which is nestled in the Galilean mountains about fifteen miles from the Sea of Galilee in the territory of the tribe of Zebulun. Jonah was a prophet of the Lord during the reign of Jeroboam II (784-743 B.C.E.). Jeroboam II, who did evil in the sight of the Lord (2 Kgs. 14:24), ruled the northern kingdom of Israel during a long period of peace and prosperity.

The reason for Israel's peace and prosperity during the time of Jonah and the reign of Jeroboam II was the political strife within the dominant power of the region—the Assyrian empire. Assyria's internal discord created a power vacuum, allowing Jeroboam II to expand his borders from the Dead Sea to the "entrance of Hamath" and to reclaim the territory lost during the reign of King Jehu (843-816 B.C.E.) and his son Jehoahaz (816-800 B.C.E.), who had been vassals of the king of Assyria (2 Kgs. 10:32-33; 13:1-9). As a prophet, Jonah successfully served King Jeroboam as a theological counselor on political and military matters, helping to reestablish Israel's boundaries (2 Kgs. 14:25).

Some scholars have claimed that Jonah was the nameless son

of Zarephath's widow (1 Kgs. 17), who was raised from the dead by the prophet Elijah;[1] others have maintained that he was a disciple of Elijah;[2] still others have insisted that after Elijah's ascension to heaven, Jonah became a disciple of Elisha, eventually becoming the unnamed prophet (mentioned in 2 Kgs. 9:1-10) who was sent by Elisha to anoint King Jehu.[3] Only one thing is certain: the word of YHWH came to Jonah, saying, "Go at once to Nineveh, that impressively large city, the center of empire, and denounce it for their evil which has come up before me."

Nineveh, the capital of Assyria,[4] was located on the east bank of the Tigris River, some five hundred miles to the east of the Israelite territory.[5] Legend has it that the mighty hunter Nimrod, the first potentate on earth, journeyed to the land of Shinar,[6] where he founded Babel. From there he continued to Assyria and built Nineveh (Gen. 10:11-12). Assyria experienced unprecedented growth and prosperity during the reigns of Ashurnasirpal II (883-859 B.C.E.) and Shalmaneser III (858-824 B.C.E.), becoming a powerful empire whose hegemony in the region both shocked and awed the surrounding nations. But by the time of Jonah, Assyria was in a post–golden age. The state was clearly in decline, rocked by internal rebellions, as provincial rulers harnessed greater political power at the expense of the Assyrian crown, even though nominal allegiance to the monarch was still professed. In 745, about a generation after Jonah, Tiglath-Pileser III (745-727 B.C.E.) would seize the throne and reverse the decline, ushering in a new climactic phase in which almost the entire Near East was brought under Assyria's sway. Tiglath-Pileser III once

---

[1] Midrash Shocher Tov 26:7.

[2] Babylonian Talmud, *Sanhedrin* 113a.

[3] PdRE 10. PdRE is the acronym for *Pirkei d'Rabbi Eliezer,* the midrashic work of the first century that has been attributed to Rabbi Eliezer ben Hyrcanus.

[4] In reality, during the time of Jonah, Nineveh ceased being Assyria's capital. Although Ashurnasirpal II (883-859 B.C.E.) and Shalmaneser III (858-824 B.C.E.) held court there in the ninth century, Nineveh would not regain the status of capital until 705 under the rule of Sennacherib (704-681 B.C.E.).

[5] The present city of Mosul in Iraq, some 250 miles north of Baghdad, is the site of the once powerful Nineveh.

[6] Present-day Iraq.

again centralized royal power and reorganized the military to move beyond conquest purely for the sake of spoils. Through a process of regime change, Assyria created an empire of provinces and vassal states. A new policy of resettlement was adopted according to which, after merciless conquest, the conquered population was deported and conscripted to forced labor on one of the multiple building projects occurring throughout the empire. This would eventually be the fate of the northern kingdom of Israel in 724 B.C.E. (2 Kgs. 17:1-23). Simultaneously, the southern kingdom of Judah would also become a vassal of Assyria. By 680, under Esarhaddon (680-669 B.C.E.), the Assyrian empire reached the zenith of its power.

Assyria's lust for power was fostered by its patron god, Assur, who craved supremacy over every other deity in the region. Developing an effective and efficient military organization became the chief occupation of the Assyrian king and state (Grayson 1991, 217). All other interests were subordinate to Assyria's military-industrial complex. In this setting, Nineveh's military establishment was the center of savage and often sadistic power. If enemies resisted surrender during the siege of their city, once defeated, the population would be horribly mutilated and slaughtered. Their houses and towns would be torn down and burned, and the flayed skins of their corpses prominently displayed on stakes: a strong warning to others who might think of resisting (Grayson 1991, 221). Public amusement was provided by leading survivors by a leash attached to a ring inserted through their lip. Vanquished nobles were paraded through the city of Nineveh with the decapitated heads of their princes hanging around their necks while merry tunes were played to entertain the public (Læssøe 1963, 96-114; Olmstead 1951, 124-205; Parrot 1955, 30-75). Is it any wonder that the Hebrews despised the people of the empire?

Assyria was not some nation with which Israelites had religious disagreement; rather, it was an evil empire, the mortal enemy of Israel, whose fundamental purpose was to destroy Jonah's people, the Israelite nation, and its way of life. For the marginalized Israelites, Nineveh came to symbolize violence and cruelty. Radak's commentary on the prophets could summarize

Nineveh's sin in two words: robbery and oppression.[7] The writings of future prophets show that contempt for Nineveh spanned several generations. Zephaniah dreamed of the day when it would be Assyria's turn to fall into ruins, with the city of Nineveh becoming a wasteland (2:13-15). Likewise, the prophet Nahum could not contain his jubilation over his prophecy that Nineveh would be destroyed.[8] He asked if anyone had escaped the unrelenting cruelty of the empire, and compared Nineveh's bloodthirsty lust to the debauchery of a whore. Nahum unapologetically rejoiced that Nineveh would suffer the humiliation of having YHWH lift up her skirt over her face to show her nakedness and shame to all the world while being pelted by YHWH with manure (Nah. 3:4-6, 19).[9]

Paradoxically, as hinted in the Midrash Yonah, the salvation of the Ninevites would usher in Israel's ultimate fall, becoming "a rod of YHWH's wrath."[10] A message to Israel was implicit in YHWH's message to Nineveh. If a wicked pagan nation would heed Jonah's proclamations and repent, thus earning the Almighty's everlasting mercies, an accusatory finger could then be pointed at the recalcitrant nation of Israel—a people who claimed to be followers of YHWH. Nineveh's repentance would become Israel's condemnation. How could Israel's obduracy allow it to remain secure after Nineveh's repentance? Could oppressors be more receptive to YHWH's word than the marginalized? If, indeed Ninevites repented, would YHWH not be justified in pouring YHWH's wrath upon Israel for failing to show a similar spirit? Briefly stated, Israel would be condemned by contrast.

---

[7] Radak 3:8. Radak is the acronym for Rav David Kimchi, an early thirteenth-century French grammarian and commentator on the prophets.

[8] The prophecy was fulfilled by 612 B.C.E., when the city was burned to the ground.

[9] The prophecy of Nahum raises an interesting question. If Nahum, who is a contemporary of either King Jotham (756-741 B.C.E.) or King Manasseh (696-642 B.C.E.), postdates Jonah, why then is there a need for a prophecy concerning the destruction of Nineveh if her people had already repented during Jonah's earlier mission to that city?

[10] Midrash Yonah, Is 10:5.

Additionally, if Nineveh were to repent, Jonah could be accused of false prophecies. After all, does not the Deuteronomist warn that if a prophet speaks in the name of the Lord, and the prophecy does not come to pass, then that person is a false prophet (Deut. 18:21-22)? Or worse, would not the wicked conclude that YHWH lacked the power to carry out YHWH's decree, mistaking his mercy for impotence?

CHAPTER 1:
JONAH'S CALL TO GO TO NINEVEH

Jonah contemplated YHWH's call, realizing that, with the exception of Elisha, who also proclaimed YHWH's word to an enemy of Israel (2 Kgs. 8:9-15), he would be the only prophet sent to proclaim the word of YHWH in a foreign land. Most other prophets denounced foreign powers from the safety of their borders. While some other prophets called by YHWH may have initially recoiled from their call, like Moses (Exod. 3:11; 4:10, 13), Gideon (Judg. 6:13), and Jeremiah (Jer. 1:6), they protested in words only, for danger existed in disobeying YHWH through actions: "For if the Lord YHWH has spoken, who can but prophesy?" (Amos 3:8). The last prophet to ignore YHWH's call was eaten by a lion (1 Kgs. 13:7-32). Even though YHWH's calling of Jonah implied that YHWH was no tribal deity localized to the land of the Hebrews, but was concerned with holding far-off kingdoms like Nineveh ethically accountable, Jonah chose to be unfaithful to YHWH. But was his unfaithfulness to YHWH a product of his faithfulness to Israel? By fleeing, was he living up to his name, "ben Amittai," which means "son of faithfulness," or failing to live up to it?

Jonah chose Tarshish as his destination, as far away as possible from what he thought was the presence of YHWH, a place that had not yet heard of YHWH's fame nor seen YHWH's glory (Isa. 66:19). Although Jonah was well aware that YHWH was able to reach the remotest parts of the earth, he hoped at least to flee from YHWH's prophetic calling. The trading city of Tarshish was believed to be situated at the other end of the known world, the geographical antipode of Nineveh. Tarshish, or Tartessos, was a former Greek colony at the estuary of the river Guadalquiver, beyond Gibraltar, located on the southwest coast of modern-day Spain.[11] According to the Mishnah,[12] it took a full year of sea travel to arrive at Tarshish. To get there, Jonah had first to descend to the seaport of Joppa[13] where he found a ship preparing to depart for Tarshish. There are those who claim that Jonah was so impatient to get under way that he paid the fare for the entire passenger load, even the empty berths.[14] His anxiety to set sail was so great that he paid the price for passage in advance, rather than afterward as was the custom of the day (Lacocque and Lacocque 1981, 40). Once the travel arrangements were made, Jonah boarded the ship for Tarshish, sailing west rather than riding east.

The ship Jonah boarded was a sturdy vessel designed for long journeys. It was probably constructed of fir planks, with a mast of cedar, linen sails, and a pine deck, and was powered by oars made of oak (Ezek. 27:5-12). Although it was a sturdy ship, Yhwh hurled an impressively great and furious wind onto the sea, causing a storm that could destroy such a vessel. The mariners were afraid and cried out to their own gods. They hurled their cargo overboard, as if trying to appease the sea with the sacrifice of their goods. Some have claimed that they also threw their useless, unresponsive idols into the sea.[15] In reality, they hoped to lighten their load to make the ship more manageable. Jonah was unaware of the turmoil occurring on the deck

---

[11] Although some scholars locate Tarshish on the southwest coast of Spain, others associate Tarshish with Tarsus, located on the southeastern coast of Asia Minor to the west of Cyprus and Greece. Still others insist that it remains an unknown location referred to in the biblical text for its association with sea commerce (see 1 Kgs. 10:22; 2 Chr. 9:21; Isa. 23:1, 14, 60:9; and Ezek. 27:25).

[12] Baba Batra 3:2.

[13] Present-day Jaffa, a suburb of Tel Aviv.

[14] Babylonian Talmud, *Nedarim* 38a.

[15] Radal on PdRE 10; 31. Radal is the acronym for Rav David Luria, the nineteenth-century Lithuanian scholar of the Torah and commentator on PdRE.

above, for he had descended to the recesses of the ship. There he fell into a deep sleep as secure as a fetus in a mother's womb.[16]

When the ship's captain discovered Jonah sleeping, he awoke him by yelling, "What is it with you? Arise, O sound sleeper! Cry out to your god! Perhaps the god in whom you believe will take notice of us and not leave us to perish!" But as the captain pleaded with Jonah to pray, the spokesperson for YHWH uttered not one word. Even though a prayer of repentance could have stopped the implacable tempest and saved his life and those of his fellow passengers, Jonah remained silent.

Making no headway against the squalling storm, the mariners spoke among themselves, and decided to cast lots to discover who had caused the evil that had befallen them. The casting of lots was a time-honored process for outing guilty parties, whether it was Achan, who knowingly violated YHWH's ban on obtaining booty (Josh. 7), or Jonathan, who inadvertently violated the oath made by his father, King Saul, during the Michmash campaign (1 Sam. 14:24-46). When the mariners cast the lots, Jonah was indicated.

Immediately they questioned Jonah. "Please tell us why this evil has occurred to us? What is your mission? Where do you come from? What is your country? Who are your people?" Jonah replied by saying, "I am a Hebrew, and YHWH, the God of the heavens is the God I fear. For YHWH made both the sea and the dry land and has power over them." Thus, Jonah confessed the very God from whom he was fleeing. Upon hearing this, the mariners were filled with fear. They asked, "What have you done? And more important, what are we to do with you so as to return calm to the sea?" for the storm was growing stronger. Jonah replied, "Lift me up and hurl me into the sea. Then will the

---

[16] Psychologist Erich Fromm interprets the prophet's finding refuge in the inner parts of the ship while others struggled for their lives as Jonah's inability to communicate properly with others. To be sound asleep in the midst of chaos symbolizes a "safe" withdrawal from the presence of others, like a fetus in a mother's womb. According to Fromm, Jonah's experience of seeking protection and isolation becomes a recurring motif of the story—repeated also in the great fish's belly (1951, 21-23).

sea be calmed for you, for I know that it is on my account that this storm rages against you." Even now, when repentance could have brought an end to the storm, Jonah chose death rather than obedience to the call of YHWH.

Perhaps Jonah thought that death by drowning—a form of asphyxiation—was a proper penalty, for custom dictated asphyxiation by the hands of heaven for those who withheld knowledge.[17] Either way, the mariners at first refused to grant Jonah's death wish. Instead, they dug into the waters with their oars in the vain hope of bringing the ship to dry land. But they were unable to, for the sea grew even worse. Finally, they did what Jonah, until now, had refused to do: they called upon YHWH. How pathetic: the pagan mariners' submissiveness before YHWH was exceeded only by the anointed prophet's stubbornness. Nevertheless, the Hebrew prophet of YHWH, who fled from YHWH's call to proclaim good news to the pagans, was still able, against his will, to bring non-Israelites to call on the name of the living God. The mariners cried out, "O YHWH, please do not let us perish on account of this man's life. And do not hold us guilty of innocent blood. For you, O YHWH, have done as it pleased you." With that, they lifted up the recalcitrant prophet and hurled him into the sea in hope that through the death of this one person, all might be saved. At that moment, the sea stood still and ceased raging. And fearing a great fear of YHWH, the mariners sacrificed sacrifices, and they vowed vows.[18]

CHAPTER 2:
JONAH IN THE BELLY OF THE WHALE

Unbeknownst to the mariners who sailed away on calm waters, YHWH had already designated an impressively great fish to swallow Jonah—not to punish him but to save him. Although condemned to drown for fleeing from YHWH's presence, Jonah

---

[17] Babylonian Talmud, *Sanhedrin* 89a; *Sukkah* 53b.

[18] The last verse of the first chapter is one of the only places in scripture where a threefold *figura etymologica* is employed (Golka 1988:87).

was saved by a miracle. Still, Jonah found himself in the belly of a gender-confused fish[19] for three days and three nights—three days and three nights, according to Near Eastern mythology, was the time required to journey to the underworld (Landes 1967, 446-50). While rescued from drowning, Jonah began to realize, with the passing of each day, that he was trapped in a limbo where the doors of escape—to death or to life—were locked and could be opened only with the key of prayer. So, finally, from the entrails of the fish, Jonah was forced to do what the ship's captain originally asked him to do—to call upon his god. But rather than offering a prayer of entreaty that would encompass regret, repentance, and hopefully reconciliation, Jonah offered up a psalm of thanksgiving and avoided dealing with the reason for his predicament.

Jonah prayed to YHWH his God by saying, "I cried out to YHWH from my distress, and YHWH answered me. From the belly of Hell I cried for help and you, O Lord, heard my voice. For you hurled me into the abyss, into the heart of the seas, as currents engulfed me and all your waves and billows washed over me." In reality, the mariners were the ones who hurled Jonah into the sea in obedience to his request. But such facts are conveniently forgotten as Jonah placed the blame for his predicament upon YHWH, whom he accused of being the agent that hurled him from the ship. Jonah continued his prayer by alleging "I am cast out from your sight! However, I will again gaze upon your holy Temple." Again Jonah blamed YHWH, this time for his banishment. In reality, YHWH did not cast him out—Jonah fled. Jonah resumed, "Water encompassed me, the deep surrounded me, seaweed was wrapped around my head. I descended to the bases of the mountains, the earth with her bars closed upon me forever. But you

---

[19] In vv. 1 and 11, the noun dāg, the masculine form for fish, is used to describe the beast that swallowed Jonah. However, in v. 2, the noun employed is dāgâ, the feminine form for fish. The Midrash Yonah attempts to reconcile the gender discrepancy by stating that the first fish to swallow Jonah was male. For three days Jonah was in his spacious belly refusing to pray. God then had the male fish spit Jonah into a female fish, one who was pregnant with 365,000 fry. The pain of close quarters finally led Jonah to his knees.

brought my life up from the pit, O YHWH my God. When my body and soul fainted within me, I remembered YHWH and my prayer came to you, into your holy Temple."

Even though the pagan mariners who hurled him into the sea proved to be more attuned to YHWH, and even though Jonah found himself in the entrails of the fish because he refused to bring YHWH's message to the pagan nation of Assyria, he could not help himself from using religious jargon to justify his actions. "Those who pay heed to the vanities of idolatry," he continued, "forsake their grace." But indeed, YHWH is offering grace to the idolaters of Nineveh, in spite of the fact that they bow their knees to Assur and follow sinful ways. After all, in the knowledge that they were sinners, YHWH sent to them his prophet Jonah, so that they might be saved. If the people of Nineveh are lost from YHWH's grace, it is not because they are sinners but because those who live on the margins of empire refused to reach out to them with YHWH's good news.

The next step for Jonah is to try to appease YHWH by offering to perform religious acts. He continues, "But I, with a loud voice of thanksgiving, will sacrifice to you; I will fulfill that which I have vowed." Throughout his pious-sounding prayer, Jonah never repents or states why he fled from YHWH. Even though no mention is made of Nineveh or of Jonah's desertion of YHWH's calling, YHWH still delivers him. In the end, Jonah is forced to acknowledge the truth about the mercy of YHWH by closing his psalm with the recognition, "Salvation comes from YHWH!" And YHWH commanded the fish, who, either out of obedience to YHWH or simply nauseated by Jonah's saccharine speech, vomited Jonah onto dry land.

CHAPTER 3:
JONAH'S MISSION IN NINEVEH

After Jonah was belched up by the great fish onto dry ground and stripped of all dignity, the word of YHWH came to him a second time: "Get up, go at once to Nineveh, that impressively great city, the center of empire, and proclaim to [not against] them the proclamation as I told you to do."[20] So Jonah rose up and went to Nineveh, in obedience to the word of YHWH.

Nineveh was an impressively great city that required a journey of three days to traverse.[21] For three days Jonah walked up and down the streets of Nineveh proclaiming YHWH's proclamation. For the first and only time in biblical history, a prophet of YHWH walked down the streets of a non-Jewish city proclaiming a message from the Lord. In a language foreign to the inhabitants, he cried out, "Forty days and Nineveh shall be overthrown!" Consisting of only five Hebrew words, this was, no doubt, the shortest prophetic message recorded in the biblical text. Jonah's message was neither an ultimatum nor a warning, but simply a declaration of doom (Sasson 1990, 267). He could have worn a sandwich board as he made his way through the imperial capital. Written on the front would be "Repent! The End Is Near!" And on the back possibly "Forty Days and Counting." Even though Jonah's message did not contain a call to believe, the Ninevites understood the intent. It was not Jonah whom they believed but the God who sent Jonah. They proclaimed a fast and, from the greatest even to the least, they put on sackcloth.

The message was accepted in spite of the messenger. Some have claimed that the Ninevites were quick to repent because the

---

[20] "Proclaim the proclamation" is another instance of the author using a *figura etymologica* (Golka 1988, 101).

[21] Attempts have been made by scholars to reconcile the size of Nineveh as depicted by the author of Jonah with the archaeological evidence, which suggests a much smaller city. If the Assyrian king Sennacherib (704-681 B.C.E.) enlarged the city from a circumference of about three miles to about seven, as modern archaeological surveys confirm, then it would not take three days to traverse the city; this would be a gross exaggeration (Madhloum 1967, 77). Attempting to explain this discrepancy, some scholars have developed a "Greater Nineveh" or "Assyrian Triangle" hypothesis, which states that when Jonah mentioned Nineveh, he was really referring to an area that encompassed surrounding cities, including Dur Sharrukin (Khorsabad) and Calah (Nimrud). However, Dur Sharrukin was not built, nor was Nineveh the capital of Assyria for at least a quarter of a century after Jonah's supposed lifetime (Bolin 1997, 35). Thus, it can be argued that Jonah proclaimed God's message *while* walking up and down all the streets and alleys of Nineveh. But even then, would this process have taken three full days?

sailors who endured the storm with Jonah went on to Nineveh and told how they had cast him into the sea only to see him miraculously rescued.[22] Or maybe the receptiveness of the Ninevites was primed by the severe earthquakes that occurred during the reign of Jeroboam II (Amos 1:1), or the full solar eclipse that astronomical calculations indicated occurred in the year 763 B.C.E. (Simon 1999, xvii-xviii). Either way, events such as these must have appeared to be heavenly signs that reinforced Jonah's warning.[23]

The word proclaimed by Jonah touched even the king of Nineveh. Unlike King Jeroboam of Israel, the pagan Ninevite king arose from his throne, removed his robes, put on sackcloth, and sat in ashes. Sackcloth was usually woven from goats' hair to create a thick coarse cloth; wearing sackcloth symbolized the rejection of all earthly comforts and pleasure. The king then proclaimed to Nineveh, "By decree of the king and his nobles: No humans or beast, herd or flock, shall taste anything. They shall not be allowed to feed, nor allowed to drink water. But let humans and beasts be covered with sackcloth.[24] And let them call to God with strength. And let each person turn from their evil way, and from the violence that is in their palms. Who knows, perhaps God may repent and turn away from God's fierce anger, so that we might not perish." And all did as the king commanded. From old men to infant girls, all wore sackcloth, with none partaking of food or drink. Even the cows in pastures wore sackcloth, as did the chickens in the coop. It seemed that even the animals of Nineveh had a clearer understanding of repentance and obedience to YHWH's words than the humans who resided in Israel on the margins of empire.

---

[22] Radak; Ibn Ezra. Rav Avraham Ibn Ezra was a great biblical commentator (as well as poet, philosopher, grammarian, and astronomer) of the early twelfth century from Toledo, Spain.

[23] It is important to note that no connection exists in the biblical text between these events and Jonah's proclamation in Nineveh.

[24] The custom of issuing a decree in the name of both the king and his nobles requiring everyone, including the animals, to wear sackcloth as sign of mourning was developed much later, during Persian period (Bickerman 1965, 250n67).

When God saw how the Ninevites had turned from their evil ways,[25] God repented of the evil that would destroy the Ninevites and did not unleash it. For has YHWH not declared, "The instant I speak about plucking up, breaking down, or destroying a nation or a kingdom, I will repent of the evil that I thought of doing to it if that nation, against whom I have spoken, would turn from their evil" (Jer. 18:7-8). Would not YHWH have spared the wicked city of Sodom from being overthrown if only ten righteous individuals had been found within her borders (Gen. 18:22-32)? For YHWH is indeed a gracious and compassionate God who does not enjoy seeking death for the wicked, but rather provides them with life if only they repudiate their evil ways (Ezek. 18:23). God's ultimate hope is that the prophet's message makes punishment unnecessary. For God does not want any to perish, but rather wants all to come to repentance (2 Pet. 3:9). Thus, in a very real sense, the city was overturned—not with the destruction that was once visited upon Sodom and Gomorrah, but with repentance.[26] But although the city's inhabitants repented, there is no evidence that their repentance was long-lasting, nor does evidence exist of a conversion to Yahwism. Still, at this point in time, repentance was enough.

CHAPTER 4:
JONAH'S ANGER OVER NINEVEH'S SALVATION

Jonah was indignant with the turn of events and fell into a rage. He was repelled by a God who "cheapened" mercy in order to spare oppressors. Thus, as YHWH's wrath ended, Jonah's wrath began. Jonah prayed to YHWH, saying, "Please, O YHWH, was this not what I said would happen when I was still in my own land?" Finally the truth came out. Jonah continued, "For this rea-

---

[25] No records exist in the Assyrian archives, or any other records of the empire, that describe the events recorded in the Book of Jonah of Nineveh's repentance before the God of Israel. Nor does any future prophet of God who prophesied against Assyria seem to know of these events; none speaks of Jonah's adventures.

[26] Babylonian Talmud, *Sanhedrin* 89b.

son, I at first fled to Tarshish, for I knew that you are a gracious and compassionate God who is slow to anger and possessing great amounts of grace. You are one who repents from punishing." Jonah abhorred YHWH's divine mercy when it is extended to Israel's archenemy, yet liberally bestowed upon him while in the belly of the fish. How dare YHWH not punish the oppressors in the way in which they deserved? How dare God upset the divine plan of retributive justice by making grace universally available? Does YHWH not stand in solidarity with the marginalized over against those of the empire whose privilege comes at the expense of the oppressed? Should not the marginalized expect their God to punish such evildoers?

If God refuses to punish Nineveh as they deserve to be punished, what hope exists that the universe is based on any type of "moral" principles? Who can live in a universe where evildoers can be redeemed? Does any justice exist within God? Who would want to live in a world where the God of justice refuses to mete out retributive justice? It is not a surprise, then, that Jonah wanted no part of a world without what he perceived to be a just God. "And now, O YHWH," he cries out, "please take my life from me. For better is my death than my life." It is ironic that, like the prophet Elijah, Jonah prayed for death. But while Elijah's death wish was due to his failure as a prophet to lead a king to repentance (1 Kgs. 19:4), Jonah's was based on his success.

YHWH responded to Jonah by asking, "Do you have a right to be angry?" Rather than answering YHWH's question, Jonah withdrew to a hillside east of the city and made for himself a *sukkâ*.[27] Constructing the booth was a subtle reminder of the covenant YHWH made with God's chosen people—in effect, those for whom God made a preferential option (Exod. 19:4-5). After all, Nineveh was like Egypt of an earlier time, an empire that sought the annihilation of the Hebrew people. Jonah sat in the shade of his booth, waiting to see what would happen to the city. When the *sukkâ* did not provide shade and protection for Jonah, the

---

[27] *Sukkôt* (pl.) are booths, reminiscent of those built in the desert during the exodus (Lev. 23:43).

Lord Y<small>HWH</small> appointed a plant to grow.[28] And it grew quickly, rising up over Jonah to shade his head and save him from discomfort. Jonah rejoiced over the plant and was very happy until the next day, when the Lord appointed a worm to attack the plant so that it withered. Later as the sun shone, the Lord appointed an east wind, a scorching sirocco, and the sun beat down so hard on Jonah's head that he fainted. Again he asked for death, saying, "Better is my death than my life."

But the Lord said to Jonah, "Is it right for you to be angry over a plant?" And Jonah replied, "Yes, angry enough to die!" Then Y<small>HWH</small> continued, "You had compassion on the plant for which you did not labor, nor did you it make grow—coming into being in a night and perishing in a night. Should I not have compassion on the impressively great city Nineveh in which there are more than a hundred and twenty thousand people who do not know between the right and the left hand, that is, between good and evil?[29] Not to mention the cattle?"

What an unanswerable question! Any response Jonah might make would betray his lack of mercy. After all, he held no right to the shade provided by the plant appointed by Y<small>HWH</small> in the first place, for it was a gift freely given by its creator. Likewise, Y<small>HWH</small> was free not only to repent of anger, but free also to offer pardon. If Jonah could show concern for a plant, could not Y<small>HWH</small> show concern for an entire city?

On the other hand, if Jonah was instead to insist on his right to be angry, then he would have to justify that anger. Surely, if Y<small>HWH</small> was expected to act with love toward Jonah, then Jonah

---

[28] The plant is referred to as קִיקָיוֹן, and is usually translated as "gourd." Although its identity is uncertain, biblical scholars have suggested that the plant could be a castor-oil plant or a quick-growing *ricinus*.

[29] A population of 120,000 appears reasonable for an ancient city with a circumference of approximately three to seven miles as described in n. 21 (Simons 1959, 527). Some scholars estimate that during the reign of Sennacherib (704-681 B.C.E.), this figure would have increased to 300,000 (Wolff 1977, 175). Still, the 120,000 figure is impressive when compared with Jerusalem, whose own population swelled to 24,000 inhabitants shortly after the fall of Israel (Broshi 1974, 23-24).

could not deny YHWH from acting with love toward others—even the Ninevites. And the account of Jonah ends at this point. We do not know how Jonah responded to YHWH, but it really doesn't matter. Any response Jonah could give would only confirm God's prerogative to act for and show mercy as YHWH chooses.

RETHINKING THE STORY OF JONAH

Jonah's story is more than a children's fairy tale of a man-swallowing whale. For the inhabitants of the empire, and those who live on the underside of the empire's power, Jonah's story is uncomfortable and disturbing. But this is what makes the story rich, for in the end, God's understanding of justice and mercy overturns preconceived assumptions.

The story of Jonah is a tale of an evil and oppressive empire that has achieved great wealth, power, and privilege at the expense of the surrounding marginalized communities. It is a story of a rebellious prophet from the empire's margins who wants only to see his oppressors utterly destroyed and who is angry with an unjust God who has shown mercy to the enemy. It is the story of a God who is quick to offer redemption and mercy even to those who deserve neither. In short, it is a story of reconciliation that encompasses God, the oppressors, and the disenfranchised. This story had as much relevance in the ancient world as it has in the modern world of today. But what does it say about us today? What can we learn from it? What does it call us to do? It is to these questions that we now turn our attention.

2

Who Was Jonah?
What Was Nineveh?

"THE MESSAGE GOD WANTS us to derive from the book of Jonah is that we who have been richly blessed have a responsibility to evangelize all the world for the glory of Jesus Christ." With these words my Sunday School teacher began to explain the importance of Jonah's story. As a young man in my twenties, I was not familiar with the narrative (nor the Bible itself), save for some cartoons that alluded to a man-swallowing whale. He continued:

> We are the spiritual Israel and an entire world full of pagans, people like the Assyrians, who do not know God nor follow His ways, are simply waiting for us Christians here in the U.S.A. to come to their lands and proclaim the Good News. But Jonah was a bad evangelist because he refused God's calling, running instead in the opposite direction. How many of you are ignoring God's calling today? Running from the Lord? But God would not let Jonah off the hook. God summoned a whale to swallow Jonah and bring him back to complete his mission.

He then told us how common it was in maritime history for sailors to fall off ships and be swallowed by a whale, only to be discovered several hours later alive in the whale's belly. One such story revolved around a whaling ship called *Star of the East*. In

1891, some two hundred miles east of the Falkland Islands in the South Atlantic, a sailor named James Bartley fell off the ship and was swallowed by a large sperm whale. Some fifteen hours later the whale was caught and killed by Bartley's shipmates. When they cut open the whale, they found Bartley alive but unconscious. With his skin bleached by the gastric acids of the whale, he was miraculously alive. Bartley retired from the whaling trade and settled down to the life of a cobbler in his native city of Gloucester, England and died eighteen years later. On his tombstone is written: "James Bartley—1870-1909: A Modern Jonah."

Having felt he had proven that humans can survive being swallowed by whales, even though the fish story about Bartley has proven somewhat difficult to document, my teacher continued his lesson.

> Although Jonah preached a sorry sermon, people still responded, repented, and came to salvation, proving God's word never comes back void. It wasn't anything Jonah said that saved the multitudes, but rather, it was God who was able to reach the heathens in spite of the reluctant prophet. This then is what we can learn from Jonah. God is calling us Americans to go out among the pagans of the world, the dark continent of Africa, the idolatrous papist nations of Latin America, and the exotic Far East to let them know of God's anger and the impending wrath that await them. Only through repentance can salvation be gained. But if we run away like Jonah, then God has no one to send, they will not hear God's message, and we, basically, condemn them to Hell.

The Book of Jonah has traditionally been reinterpreted— particularly in more conservative settings—as an evangelical call for those who live in the light to bring good news to those who live in darkness. Nevertheless, the story remains popular with children, both within and outside of the church. But is this the *only* interpretation of the story of Jonah? What might other readings indicate? For example, what would we hear if we read the story of Jonah through a liberationist lens? What if Jonah were read from the perspective of marginalized people, those without power?

To begin, we must first understand who exactly the characters are and what the story is actually about. And any liberationist reading must examine questions of power: Is there a dominating power within the story? And is there a group that exists on the margins of that power? We quickly discover that those with power in the story of Jonah were the Ninevites who inhabited the capital of the powerful Assyrian empire. Jonah and the Israelites, along with many other peoples, were marginalized and were destined to fall before Assyria's armies within a generation of the story's setting. So, contrary to my Sunday School teacher's reading, Jonah and the Israelites would not represent the United States, the most powerful nation the world has ever witnessed. Similarly, the Assyrians were the conquerors, rather than a people in some distant place waiting to hear the good news of their salvation. There are clear sociopolitical parallels that link the United States with the empire of Assyria, and Jonah and Israel represent those who exist at the margins of the empire and are subject to its mercy or domination. The Jonah story, then, becomes a story of the oppressed called upon to approach their oppressors with a message from the Lord.

Like all biblical stories, the story of Jonah was originally told, and retold, and eventually recorded within a particular culture, in a particular geographic location, and at a particular point in time. However, most biblical stories, including the story of Jonah, incorporate universal lessons that go beyond one culture, one place, or one era. This chapter will examine the structures of power at play in the time of the Assyrian empire along with the structures of power within the socio-political context of our twenty-first century. To understand these structures of power, we must begin by observing the historical, economic, and political factors that led to our present social context of the powerful and the powerless, the enfranchised and the disenfranchised, the rich and the poor. How are these dualities tied to the rise of the U.S. empire?

This new reading through a liberationist lens will undoubtedly challenge the interpretation of my former Sunday School teacher, as well as all other traditional readings. We have grown up hearing Jonah's story and it has become too familiar. We hear a call to evangelize nonbelievers rather than a challenge to holders of power.

A HISTORY OF TODAY'S ASSYRIAN EMPIRE

Are we justified in talking about the United States as an empire? Surely, many—whether conservatives or liberals—will bristle at such terminology. After all, how could the United States, the "city on the hill," to use a Reaganesque phrase, hamper anyone's else freedom? U.S. military campaigns are conducted with the noble purpose of bringing liberty to the oppressed living under dictatorial rule or in a crusade against the forces of evil or terrorism. As the torchbearers of democracy, how could we possibly be compared to the Assyrian empire? Surely the use of the word "empire" must be either hyperbole or part of a "blame America first" way of thinking. Although using the word "empire" to describe the United States may cause discomfort among the privileged and powerful, it is still crucial to recognize the power structures that exist in the world today. The United States represents a dominant culture to the rest of the world, but even within this country there are the dominating and the dominated. The United States has an underside of marginalized people whose voices need to be heard. If we want to reduce and eventually eliminate distinctions between dominating and dominated, reconciliation between the groups must occur and the use of language must recognize structures of power.

By using the term "empire," we recognize that the concept of empire is no longer limited to physically possessing foreign lands that are forced to pay tribute. While empires of old were defined by how much land their armies could control, today's empires are more often based on economic control. Physical troops stationed on foreign lands cease to be necessary, except under certain circumstances where "nation building" is required. Indeed, "nation building" is commonly a euphemism for reorganizing nations to benefit the U.S. economy. Today's understanding of empire has evolved to encompass the globalization of the economy by one superpower to provide multinational corporations with economic benefits, with capital gains secured and protected by a military might depicted as a necessity placed in the service of justice and peace. Like the Assyrian or Roman empires of old, the United States secures a *pax americana* so that the elite leaders of the empire, and their counterparts within dominated countries, can reap the economic benefits, usually at the expense of the vast majority of the world's marginalized.

An empire, that of the Assyria of ancient days or the United States of today, can rise only through the existence of disenfranchised groups that are needed to provide both raw material and cheap labor. For Assyria, regional domination was possible because it appropriated the labor and resources of its weaker neighbors. Assyria prospered at the expense of Israel, Judah, Tyre, northern Syria, and Aram-Damascus. The wealth, prosperity, and power of the center were dependant on the exploitation of the groups of people that existed on their margins. Although the mechanics differ, the basic concept of oppressive structures responsible for the empires of old holds true for all empires since that time.

The real power of modern empires resides more in their economies. It is a given that economic structures and relationships create and heavily influence societal power relationships. Consider the example of Europe. Prior to the consolidation of power in the 1500s, Europeans were politically insignificant when compared to the Ottoman empire, China under the Ming Dynasty, or northern India under the Mongols (Kennedy 1987, 3-30). Yet, with the Age of Exploration and the colonization that followed, those who resided in what has come to be called the "third world," with their enormous human and natural wealth, provided the necessary material resources that transformed a marginalized Islamic-encircled Europe into a cluster of world powers whose dominance continues to be felt today. Non-European lands existed to enrich the center. And all too often the rise of the European empires was rooted in the murder, rape, pillage, and exploitation of those who lacked military and technological superiority. Europeans, with their weapons of mass destruction, were able to appropriate the fruits of the lands and enslave or exterminate their inhabitants. Unfortunately, military or technological superiority is often confused with cultural and/or intellectual supremacy.

The Period of Colonization

The so-called discovery of new worlds, along with the exploration of African and Asian lands, brought the concept of empire to the modern world. While no single event or date demarcates the onset of the modern concept of empire, if a date had to be chosen, it would be January 13, 1493. On that day Native American blood was first spilled in a prelude to the greatest genocide in human history (Columbus 1960, 146-49). On this day of violence, the Spanish conquest of the Americas ushered in the age of modernity. This was a deeply racialized process that developed human categories based on "visible" genotypes and skin tones to determine which groups were assigned superior mental or spiritual attributes to be rulers and which were assigned superior physical strength to provide manual labor. This first day of the European conquest of the Americas planted the seeds of underdevelopment in the soil of the so-called New World. Biblical scholar R. S. Sugirtharajah reminds us that these *conquistadores* fused biblical and historical events: God was communicated as a being who would rain down punishment upon natives, but, fortunately, the Spaniards would arrive to be their liberators and saviors. The conquerors would rescue the inhabitants of the land from the fate of God's punishment that awaited them (2001, 67).

The creation of empire through colonization, and the enslavement of peoples to generate cheap labor, created an economic system that subordinated the people of two-thirds of the world. Their precious metals and physical bodies were offered up as sacrifices to the development of a system of global capitalism. The global economic and political structures constructed during Europe's early development of capitalism created a structure of underdevelopment in the colonized nations that persists even today. Their economic surplus and material resources were expropriated in order to generate economic development in the European center.

Although the United States was constructed as a colony of the British Empire, it eventually broke away to satisfy its own greed for land. Despite the fact that American history books claim that the cause of the Revolutionary War was the desire for liberty, the quest for freedom was actually limited to white male landholders. Washington (probably the richest man in the colonies), Jefferson, Adams, Hamilton, Madison, and other Founding Fathers viewed government as the protector of property. The goals of the young republic were fully identified with the interests of the landholders. They were to rule, or, as James Madison wrote in Federalist Paper #10: "[If property owners rule then] a rage for paper money, for an abolition of debts, for an equal division of property, or for any other improper or wicked project, will be less apt to pervade the whole body of the Union than a particular member of it" (1961, 84). These patriots controlled most of the land on the Atlantic coast, as well as all aspects of political life. They then turned to land in the west belonging to the Native nations.

Certainly a motivating impulse in breaking away from England was to create a new nation, a legal entity that could assert its rights to political power, profits, and land from those who were clients of the British Empire. After the defeat of the French in the French and Indian War of 1754-1763, the British were unable to subdue the Indians, who united to protect their lands. The conflict came to be known as Pontiac's War. A peace was negotiated in 1763 that declared Indian lands west of the Appalachians off limits to the American colonists. During the peace negotiations the British gave the attacking Indian chiefs a gift of blankets taken from a smallpox hospital. This pioneering effort at "biological warfare" decimated the Native population, but the American colonies were still angered by the prohibition to take land belonging to the Native peoples. However, a new nation would no longer be bound by Britain's treaties and agreements and could begin a westward march. Not surprisingly, every important Indian nation fought with the British and against the colonists during the Revolutionary War (Zinn 2003, 59-60, 87, 125).

Manifest Destiny

For the United States to come into existence, the original inhabitants of the land were either slaughtered or evicted. The genocide of Native populations due to epidemics such as small-pox—European diseases for which the people had no immuni-ties—was interpreted as divinely sanctioned. Religious leaders such as John Winthrop understood the decimation of Indians by smallpox as God "making room" for Euroamericans by "clear-[ing their] title to this place" (Takaki 1993, 39-40).

The westward movement, in general, was also perceived as ordained by God. John O'Sullivan, editor of the *Democratic Review*, best captured this religious sentiment in coining the phrase "Manifest Destiny." He wrote of "[o]ur manifest destiny to overspread the continent allotted by Providence for the free development of our yearly multiplying millions" (1845, 5). As Israel of old was given the promised land, Euroamericans, because of their racial superiority, were entrusted with what was viewed as virgin land and were given the responsibility of taming the wilderness and physically taking possession of the entire con-tinent. As God led the wandering Israelites into the promised land, calling for the genocide of all who stood in their way (Exod. 23:23), so too would Americans as the New Israel—God's cho-sen people—violently take possession of the land occupied by modern Canaanites. If the United States represented the new Jerusalem, then part of its Manifest Destiny was to spread the Protestant gospel in order to overcome the savagery of "primitive tribes" throughout the continent and the "heresy" of Roman Catholicism in the southwest. Or, as Senator Thomas Hart Ben-ton of Missouri (senator 1821-1851) saw it, the "white" race was following the "divine command to subdue and replenish the earth" by destroying "savagery" and replacing the "wigwam" with the "Capitol," the "savage" with the "Christian," and the "red squaws" with the "white matrons"(Takaki 1993, 191). This ideology of expansion initiated the conquest of Texas and northern Mexico and extended U.S. boundaries, physically possessing and repopulating the new lands.

Manifest Destiny was not to be limited to the North American continent. The Reverend Josiah Strong, in 1885, saw the Christian responsibility of the white race to extend to all the world. He wrote:

> It seems to me that God, with infinite wisdom and skill, is training the Anglo-Saxon race for an hour sure to come in the world's future. . . . If I read not amiss, this powerful race will move down upon Mexico, down upon Central and South America, out upon the islands of the sea, over upon Africa and beyond. And can any one doubt that the result of this competition of races will be the "survival of the fittest"? (Smith 1963, 85-87).

The Spanish-American War (April-August 1898) heralded a new stage in imperialist ambitions as described by Reverend Strong. By the end of the nineteenth century, the United States had moved from an economy of competitive capitalism to one of monopolistic capitalism. This new stage of capitalism merged with imperialism and found its first expression outside the continent on the islands of Cuba (with the United State as its regent), Puerto Rico (now a colony), and the Philippines (an imperialist possession after brutal suppression of the indigenous populations). By challenging the declining empire of Spain, the United States launched its first venture in world imperialism.

As a newly established empire, now with bases in the West and East, the United States was less interested in acquiring territory than in controlling economies to obtain financial benefits for the center. Economic domination began to erase boundaries, all the while establishing relationships of dependence with the new territories, masked by the guise of their independence. This model soon spread throughout the entire Western Hemisphere under the slogans of "gunboat diplomacy" and "speaking softly but carrying a big stick." President William Howard Taft best captured the emerging empire's sentiments when he concluded, "the day is not far distant [when] the whole hemisphere will be ours in fact

as, by virtue of our superiority of race, it already is ours morally"
(Pearce 1982, 17).

As the twentieth century began, the United States had four
major groups of marginalized peoples: Native Americans, the
original occupants of the land, who had survived the genocide;
Africans, who had been brought against their will to serve as
slaves, and their descendants; Hispanics, including those from
northern Mexico who had not moved but were now part of the
United States; and Asians, who, like Africans, had been brought
as a labor force.

The twentieth century was characterized by economic expan-
sionism. Nearly every country along the Caribbean was invaded
at least once by the United States during the 1900s. The U.S. military provided support for U.S. corporations like the United Fruit
Company so they could build highways in these developing countries to extract their natural resources, most often by brute force.
These U.S.-installed "banana republics" resulted in poverty, strife,
and death in all of these countries. Not surprisingly, some of the
inhabitants of those countries, deprived of their livelihood, used
these same roads to follow their exported resources north to the
United States, following what had been stolen from them. This
brief review of a century of exploitation of Latin America sheds
new light on the immigration "problem" the United States faces
today.

ECONOMIC IMPERIALISM AND
THE BIRTH OF NEOLIBERALISM

Since the end of World War II, most of the former colonies in
the global South have sought and gained independence from
Eurocentric powers, often after violent struggles. In the latter
decades of the twentieth century, although colonial imperialism
has waned, economic colonization and imperialism have taken
its place. Under the former colonial system, the powers of the
world directly occupied the lands of others to extract both their
national resources and human labor to manufacture goods.
Today, the more modern form of economic global exploitation—

termed neoliberalism[1]—determines what will be produced, who (nation-state or group of individuals) will produce it, under what conditions it will be produced, what will be paid for the finished product, what will be the profits, and who will benefit from the profits. This ensures a steady flow of resources to the center of power and privilege.[2] But there is a cost. Nation states forfeit a good portion of their sovereignty as they lose the ability to regulate or control the primary factors of production and exchange, specifically money, technology, people, and goods, which now move with ease across their borders. Like the colonial structures of old, economic imperialism is a racialized project that creates a relationship in which the world's poor, who are predominantly of color, are relegated to serve a minority of white elites.

This new global form of sovereignty is what Michael Hardt and Antonio Negri call "empire" in their book by the same name. They go on to explain that "Empire establishes no territorial center of power and does not rely on fixed boundaries or barriers. It is a *decentered* and *deterritorializing* apparatus of rule that progressively incorporates the entire global realm within its open, expanding frontiers (Hardt and Negri 2000, xi-xii).

The pervasiveness and force of neoliberalism loose in the world today have created obstacles to reconciliation between the empire of the United Sates and the underdeveloped countries of the world, which are no longer able to make decisions about the use of their resources or the development of their people. The power of neoliberalism has also created obstacles to reconciliation between Euroamericans and people of color within our own

---

[1] The term "neoliberalism" was coined after the collapse of the Eastern Bloc and its barriers to a capitalist-based world market to describe the social and moral implications of global market liberalism (capitalism) and the revival of its free-trade policies (hence "neo").

[2] For example, the cost of servicing the debt of the two-thirds world was over $375 billion in 2004. This flow of resources to global banking centers is more than all monies spent in the global South on health and education, and twenty times more than is annually received in the form of foreign aid. See James S. Henry, "Where the Money Went," *Across the Board* (March/April 2004): 42-45.

borders, groups usually distinguished from each other as the powerful and the powerless. Thus, it is important to understand the economic and racist aspects of the U.S. empire, as well as the role religion plays in its systems of domination.

THE ECONOMIC FACE OF EMPIRE

It is a serious mistake to reduce oppression to simple economic disparity. Nevertheless, it should be recognized that the granting of civil and political rights with the exclusion of economic rights denies the existence of all rights. All too often, attempts are made to secure civil and political liberties without a more equitable disbursement of wealth; the only outcome, then, is legislatively provided civil and political freedom but involuntary economic servitude. Class and caste economic structures have only reinforced the racial boundaries created between the global haves and have-nots. When we consider that the approximately 9 percent of the world's population who benefit from consuming half of the world's resources are predominately white, while the nearly one billion people subsisting in absolute poverty are predominately of color, we are forced not only to question the morality of our global distribution of resources but, more important, whether reconciliation can ever be achieved between the global haves and have-nots.

Underdevelopment will persist as long as a system of neoliberalism continues to privilege the nations that control markets and resources. According to the United Nations, the transfer of capital from poor nations to rich ones was $784 billion in 2006—up from $229 billion in 2002.[3] This is why the poorest 60 percent of today's world population owns just 6 percent of the world's wealth while the richest 20 percent concentrated in industrial Western nations own 85 percent of the world's income. Moreover, those who reside on the margins of empire can never repeat the stages of economic development characteristic of so-called first-world nations. They have no global "Other" to exploit.

---

[3] Tina Rosenberg, "Reverse Foreign Aid: Why Are Poor Countries Subsidizing Rich Ones?" *New York Times*, March 25, 2007.

Neoliberalism is designed to transfer wealth, in the form of raw materials, natural resources, and cheap labor from the two-thirds world to the so-called first world. This transfer is normally enabled by what are termed "fair trade" agreements. The economic and military powers of the United States allow multinational corporations to structure agreements that benefit the elite within the empire and the dominated nation, without any obligation to the inhabitants of that nation. Sovereign nations from the two-thirds world are all too often reduced to simply observing the flow of resources, populations, commodities, and monies to the benefit of the center of power. As Cornel West reminds us, "For most of the history of the American empire, government has been a tool for preserving and furthering the power and might of white male corporate elites—a small percentage of white men in the country" (2004, 33). Resources, the birthright from weaker nations, appropriated through a "forced" open market, cause internal scarcities in what is needed to maintain any type of humane living standard. As standards of living become lower, repressive political systems are installed so the economic market system can function. The political stability needed to ensure the steady and profitable flow of goods supersedes any desire for freedom and liberty.[4]

The oppressive neoliberal economic order advocated by the United States usually wears the mask of democracy. Although striving for democracy has been claimed, the United States has overthrown other democracies (for example, Abenz in Guatemala, Allende in Chile, and Mossadegh in Iran) in order to install brutal dictators pledged to protect U.S. business interests. It has also invaded other countries using the flimsiest of excuses (Lebanon, Vietnam, Grenada, Panama, and Iraq, among others), and maintained close relationships with some of the world's most brutal dictators (Marcos in the Philippines, Suharto in Indonesia, Hussein in Iraq prior to the invasion, and the Shah of Iran, to name a few). When words like "freedom" and "liberty" are used

---

[4] Further exploration showing this transfer of wealth can be found in my earlier work *Doing Christian Ethics from the Margins*, specifically chapters 4 and 5.

today—and they have been repeated often in the context of
Iraq—they do not mean freedom or liberty for the people to
determine their own destiny; instead, they mean the freedom and
liberty that give U.S. corporations access to the markets and
resources of the world and allow them to develop structures to
ensure that this system continues.

Many of the structures put in place—such as the World Bank,
the International Monetary Fund (IMF), the North American
Free Trade Agreement (NAFTA), and the World Trade Organization (WTO)—cater to U.S. economic interests and, in effect,
legitimize the ability of a small percentage of white men in multinational corporations to control the human and natural resources
of other countries. Threats of the IMF or World Bank to withhold
credit or implement "austerity" programs are often as onerous
as an invading army. What the Assyrians were able to accomplish
with troops in the field during Jonah's time pales in comparison
to the business strategies for market domination being developed
in today's corporate boardrooms. And while the military superiority of the world's only superpower remains an important threat
kept in reserve, more is accomplished through the manipulation
of economies.

Any population or nation group that attempts to chart a destiny contrary to the economic goals of the multinational corporations automatically is suspect, thus justifying the empire's right
to intervene and impose a peace that secures markets. Security
and stability are required for resources to flow toward the center
of empire. Rivals, who are not tolerated, used to be labeled communists; today they can be labeled terrorists. For example, in
1988, a Pentagon report during the Reagan administration
labeled Nelson Mandela's African National Congress as one of
the more "notorious terrorist groups," and George H. W. Bush,
Reagan's vice president, praised Romania's Nicolae Ceauşescu
for his "respect for human rights" (Chomsky 2003, 110, 113).
The empire has divided the world into "white" hats and "black"
hats. The empire does democracy building and the "black" hats
do terrorism. Our intentions are noble and just, never to be questioned, while theirs seek to destroy us because of their hatred and
jealousy of our freedoms. The "white-hatted" empire has a moral

right to hold unquestionable power over the whole world: it is for the world's own good, even if it means temporarily limiting or interfering with the sovereignty of other nations.

Why then should we be surprised with the United States' new foreign-policy doctrine of pre-emptive strikes (even nuclear[5]), the right to initiate military operations against a country that *might* pose a possible future threat to U.S. power? Other avenues for conflict resolution, such as within worldwide institutions like the United Nations, are ignored or bypassed. "Regime change" in the new millennium seems to be a repackaging of the U.S. foreign policy toward Latin America during the first half of the twentieth century—a policy that reserved the right to determine what constituted a threat to U.S. interests and security and then to act unilaterally, whether or not an actual threat was imminent. Given this history, old and new, it not difficult to understand why "*they*" hate us so much—a hatred, no doubt, similarly held by Jonah and the people of Israel toward Assyria.

Although the U.S. empire is maintained by marginalizing the inhabitants of other lands, these oppressive structures found their inception and were modeled on the treatment of people *within* U.S. borders. The global structures that oppress Africans, Asians, Latin Americans, and aboriginal peoples around the world are rooted in what first happened to Africans and African Americans, Asians and Asian Americans, Hispanic Americans, and Native American peoples at home. While much can be said about how globalization impoverishes the vast majority of the world's population, it remains beyond the scope of this book. Instead, our focus is on marginalization within the boundaries of the U.S. empire and how reconciliation can come about between the marginalized and those with power.

---

[5] According to a classified Pentagon report presented to Congress on January 8, 2002, "the Bush administration has directed the military to prepare contingency plans to use nuclear weapons against at least seven countries and to build new smaller nuclear weapons for use in certain battlefield situations." Among the countries targeted were China, Russia, Iraq, North Korea, Syria, Iran, and Libya. See Paul Richter, "Seven Countries Named Potential Nuclear Targets for U.S.," *Miami Herald*, March 9, 2002.

Just as first-world conditions exist among the elite in the two-thirds world, two-thirds–world conditions exist in the first world. According to data released by the Internal Revenue Service, the share of U.S. income in 2005 that went to the top 1 percent of Americans (average income of $1.1 million a year) was the largest share (21.8 percent) since the eve of the Great Depression of 1929 (the peak was hit in 1928 when the top 1 percent reported 23.9 percent of all income). The top 10 percent of Americans (who average more than $100,000 a year) received 48.5 percent of the nation's income, again a share not seen since 1929. The remaining 50 percent of national income is shared by the remaining 90 percent of Americans, whose income across the board has been steadily dropping. Today, the top 300,000 Americans collectively enjoy as much of the nation's income as do the bottom 150 million Americans, which represents 440 times as much as the average person in the bottom half, a near doubling of the 1980 gap.[6] Not since the years of the robber barons has this nation seen such an intense concentration of wealth in the hands of so few individuals. In short, the rich are getting richer and the poor are getting poorer, thanks mainly to massive tax cuts to the wealthiest of Americans since the 1980s, combined with deep cuts in social services for health care, welfare, child care, and education. It should be no surprise that the poorest of the poor, those who suffer most from the transfer of wealth from the poor to the rich are disproportionately persons of color. For the U.S. economy to function efficiently, an industrial "reserve army" of laborers must always exist. This is a racialized "reserve army" disproportionately made up of people of color, as has been shown by almost every U.S. study of unemployment or underemployment.[7] No

---

[6] David Cay Johnston, "Income Gap Is Widening, Data Shows," *New York Times*, March 29, 2007.

[7] According to the official figures released by the U.S. Department of Labor, the unemployment rate for February 2007 was 4.5 percent, varying between 4.4 and 4.6 percent since September 2006. The unemployment rate among African Americans during the same period was almost double the national average at 7.9 percent. Hispanics fared a bit better at 5.2 percent, a new low (see http://www.bls.gov/news.release/empsit.nr0.htm). Yet the situation faced by men of color, specifically African Americans, is more dire

matter how one chooses to quantify the disenfranchised in the United States, research studies always point to racial and ethnic inequalities. Those who are most removed from the "white ideal" disproportionately fill our prisons, attend dilapidated schools, occupy the most menial jobs, and live in the most economically deprived neighborhoods or reservations. Park Avenue profits by the surplus extracted from Spanish Harlem; the taming of the "West" was made by corralling Native people onto reservations; Atlanta's wealth was created by the black ghettos of that city; and the households and businesses of Los Angeles thrive by utilizing "illegal immigrants." The luxury houses of the exclusive gated "vanilla" suburbs are established at considerable cost. Their privileged space protects these families from the menace of the "chocolate" urban centers, while drawing upon this marginalized space for help when needed. The term *dependency theory* is used to describe such a relationship. Just as the power and privilege of the Assyrian empire of old were dependent on surrounding marginalized communities, so too are middle- and upper-class status maintained at the expense of marginalized U.S. people of color. In addition to dependency theory, the reserve army of the underclass is systematically barred from economic opportunities that would significantly raise its status. Both exclusion and exploitation contribute to the conditions prevalent in this nation's ghettos, reservations, and *barrios*.

In the minds of some in the dominant culture, marginalized groups who continue to "choose" to live in disenfranchised conditions are blamed for their failure to take full advantage of the civil rights reforms. A commonly held belief is that if the mar-

---

than these official statistics indicate. Several scholarly studies show that the disproportion in employment has worsened. For example, 65 percent of young black men (in their twenties) without a high school diploma were without jobs in 2000. By 2004, the share had grown to 72 percent. Even with high school diplomas, half of black men in their twenties were jobless in 2004, up from 46 percent in 2000. Add to this dilemma incarceration rates that have climbed in the 1990s and reached historic levels over the past few years. It is estimated that by their mid-thirties, six in ten black men without a high school diploma have been incarcerated. See Erik Eckholm, "Plight Deepens for Black Men, Studies Warn," *New York Times*, March 20, 2006.

ginalized or underrepresented cannot make it with a "quota" system such as affirmative action, it is solely their fault. Besides, the defenders of neoliberalism insist that the economic privilege shared by the empire's elite will "trickle down" to the masses: "A rising tide lifts all boats." And while such slogans are usually associated with the U.S. "right," members of the traditional left are also defenders of neoliberalism and empire. Liberals may express, with teary eyes, guilt over the plight of the marginalized, but all too often it is done from the comfort of financial and sociopolitical security, as they remain unaware of their own complicity with oppressive social structures while professing to understand the disenfranchised social location.

To a certain extent, particularly in terms of global economic policies, it really didn't make much difference whether neoconservative George W. Bush or liberal John Kerry won the 2004 presidential election. The empire's democratic system seems reduced to choosing between two pro-empire individuals with no significant differences in their commitments to protecting the rights of multinational companies to expand globally, even at the expense of their constituents. Both would ignore that the gap between the rich and the poor more than doubled between 1980 and 2005 as the United States experienced the greatest growth in wage inequality in the Western world. Both candidates defended free-market policies, and neither would pledge to deal seriously with the undemocratic distribution of wealth, resources, and privilege.

Even if marginalized communities were to organize effectively to change the political and economic structures of the United States in order to create a more just distribution of wealth and resources, all branches of government, whether controlled by the political right or left, would unite to protect neoliberalism. Dwight Hopkins reminds us:

> If the national politics and economics were threatened with a reversal, that is, if the pyramidal monopoly capitalist structure in the United States began to move bottom to top, then the so-called checks and balances system would rally to prevent such a movement. The present system would

immediately stop the realization of genuine democracy in which the majority of the citizens—the people at the bottom in the United States—would own all the economic resources as well as the military-industrial complex, and would, therefore, control the federal government. (Hopkins 2000, 187)

In effect, Americans in general, and people of color in particular, are actually precluded from any meaningful participation in determining the country's destiny. This assures a future America with a privileged white minority because of a socio-political structure that hints strongly of apartheid. In the twenty-first century, economics will be the means by which the "color line" is drawn; the vast majority of the poor, those locked out of the economic benefits of this country, are and will be persons of color.

THE RACIST FACE OF EMPIRE

Racial classification is central to empire. Sociologist Howard Winant reminds us that,

> Not only was the concept of race born with modernity, not only was the meaning of race a preoccupation of the Enlightenment, but the racial practices of the modern age — slavery and imperial conquest, as well as abolition and anti-colonialism—shaped all the social structures we take for granted." (Winant 2004, ix)

White supremacy is woven into the very fabric of U.S. culture. Winant's definition of race as a sociohistorical construct is helpful: "Race is a concept that signifies and symbolizes sociopolitical conflicts and interests in reference to different types of human bodies." Racism, then, can be understood as "the routinized outcome of practices that create or reproduce hierarchical social structures based on essentialized racial categories." To a great extent, racism is not a matter of beliefs or intention, but can be understood only in terms of consequences (Winant 2004, x, 126). Because of the racial undergirding of empire, those who are farther away from the white ideal in skin tone can expect to live under poorer economic conditions with a shorter life span, fewer opportunities, and limited access to proper sanitation, health care, and education.

The controllers of the empire also determine who will profit financially from the blood, sweat, and tears of others. Who produces resources and how those resources are distributed happens along racial and ethnic lines. Political and social scientist Eric Williams, who went on to become the prime minister of Trinidad and Tobago, successfully argued that slavery was not created by racism but, rather, that slavery, as an economic phenomenon, produced racism. The limited European population of the sixteenth century needed free laborers to cultivate the staple crops of sugar, tobacco, and cotton in the so-called New World. Thus, slavery was necessary. As the colonizers turned first to Native Americans and then to Africans to meet this need, they morally justified the oppression of others by an ideology of white supremacy. In this way, slavery and the racialization of the Other reinforced each other (E. Williams 1944, 6-7).

As slavery created racism, it also created the modern concept of capitalism. The profits gained from the global slave trade provided England with the seed money for the Industrial Revolution. It is no coincidence that the major English port cities in which the Industrial Revolution developed were the same cities that originally profited from the slave trade. With the demise of slavery and the rise of industrialism, the need for cheap labor continued, as did the need for new and varied forms of racism. Racial inequalities survived the end of slavery and, a hundred years later, also survived the civil rights movement.

For the past five hundred years, these racial and ethnic forms of economic oppression have been seen as normative and legitimate in the eyes of the overwhelming majority of Euroamericans, an entrenched understanding that found legal and religious justification.[8] During the 1960s, the civil rights movement in the

---

[8] Eugenics, the science that deals with the improvement of hereditary qualities of a species or breed, was constitutionally upheld by the U.S. Supreme Court in the 1927 case *Buck v. Bell*.

United States (and other antiracist, anticolonial, and democratizing movements throughout the world) radically challenged the way nonwhites were seen. Nevertheless, racial hegemony was preserved by repackaging white supremacy under the concept of "color blindness." In spite of the omnipresence of racism in every aspect of U.S. life, the dominant culture began to insist on the construct of color blindness and a rhetoric of reverse discrimination.

When teaching undergraduates at a predominantly conservative Euroamerican college, I had them write a sociopolitical autobiography. Among many questions, they were asked to describe the racial and ethnic composition of their neighborhood, their school, and their church. A question further on asked them to describe what they learned from their parents about people of different races and ethnicities. The overwhelming majority of the white students wrote that they lived, worshiped, and were schooled in an environment devoid of racial and ethnic diversity. Most repeated the "politically correct" line about how they felt cheated by not experiencing diversity, and how they truly wished to interact with those who were different. However, when they later described the lessons learned from their parents about people of color, they usually made comments like, "My parents taught me to treat everyone the same"; "I was taught to be color-blind, just like God"; or "I was taught that we are all God's children and we should therefore love each other." The students failed to notice the link between the color blindness taught by their parents and the segregated life in which they were raised. Their parents must have been aware of color, because they had chosen to live in predominantly white neighborhoods. But given their claim of color blindness, they could not be bigots. In addition, they felt righteous indignation when hearing bigoted comments. These students had no need to believe in white supremacy because the racist social structures surrounding them protected their white privilege even as they lamented a lack of diversity.

The construct of color blindness ignores institutionalized racism and veils individual bigotry. Racial injustice is rationalized as the expected outcome of individuals competing on a level playing field. And occasionally a face of color is placed on a pedestal to prove that minorities who work hard enough can be as successful as white people.[9] Thus, the civil rights movement can be hailed for its success in eliminating most of our racist past and we can speak about living in a postracial world (Winant 2004, 33, 43). Or can we?

Somehow racism and ethnic discrimination persist. In fact, the radical nature of the civil rights movement was toned down in order to obtain some important concessions from the dominant culture. The more radical demands in the struggle for justice can always be weakened, if not nullified, by integrating the opposition into the movement (Gramsci 1971, 182). Even Martin Luther King's dream that his children be judged by the "content of their character," and not "the color of their skin," was co-opted by the insistence that affirmative action violates the spirit of King's "dream" and that true followers of King would advocate color blindness. As antiracist laws were enacted, the social structures that maintain and sustain racism were not fundamentally changed or transformed. The more radical demands of the civil rights movement, such as those for the equitable distribution of wealth, resources, and opportunities were sacrificed in favor of limited economic, political, and cultural access to power and privilege for a minority of middle-class people of color (Winant 2004, 21-22, 33, 43).

Shortly after the passage of civil rights legislation, working-class incomes experienced deep declines. By the close of the 1970s, median family income remained at 1973 levels as unemployment rose to 7.5 percent by 1980. The 1980s witnessed a dramatically widening income gap, while the middle class shrank, due in large part to the Reagan administration's entrenchment of neoliberal economic policies within the country, which radically changed the distribution of wealth. During the 1980s, the wealthiest 10 percent of families increased their income by 16 percent

---

[9] The nation glimpsed this attitude in the remarks made by the liberal senator from Delaware, Joseph Biden, about presidential contender Barack Obama, when Biden referred to him as "the first mainstream African-American who is articulate and bright and clean and a nice-looking guy." See Lynette Clemetson, "The Racial Politics of Speaking Well," *New York Times*, February 4, 2007.

and the top 5 percent increased theirs by 23 percent, and the top 1 percent increased their income by 50 percent. Meanwhile, the bottom 80 percent all lost money, with the poorest 10 percent losing 15 percent of their income. Reagan's action in moving the nation to a supply-side economy, which did much to dismantle the New Deal legislation, was mainly responsible for increasing the income of the top 1 percent: at the beginning of his term it was 65 times greater than the bottom 10 percent, and at the end it was 115 times greater (Phillips 1990, 12-17). According to Census Bureau figures, the richest saw their inflation-adjusted income rise by 30 percent from the late 1970s to the mid 1990s, while the poorest among us saw their income decrease by 21 percent. From 1947 through 1979, real income rose for all segments of society, but since 1980 incomes have risen only for the most affluent families (Cooper 1998, 338-54).

As this happened, the average working white American did not necessarily blame the corporate leaders who benefited from the full implementation of neoliberalism, although in 1975 these corporate leaders made 44 times as much as the average factory worker and by 1985, the average CEO salary rose to 70 times that of the average worker.[10] And that trend has continued. A 2001 report published by the Institute for Policy Studies revealed that corporate leaders were making 531 times as much as the average factory worker, a 571 percent increase (before adjusting for inflation) since 1990. Workers' pay, meanwhile, which grew 37 percent, barely outpaced inflation at 32 percent (Anderson et al. 2001, 1-6).

Corporate greed, the desire for greater profits, which led to outsourcing and downsizing, was not really examined as a cause of declining living standards; instead, resentment among the white working-class often took the form of blaming and scapegoating people of color. Affirmative action was seen by the white working class as legislation that gave blacks, Hispanics, and Asian Americans unfair advantages. "Welfare queens" and those

---

[10] David Leonhardt, "The Imperial Chief Executive Is Suddenly in the Cross Hairs," *New York Times*, June 24, 2002.

who "do not play by the rules" were conjured up as the cause of the economic downturn for working-class whites. Reverse discrimination, used to explain why whites were getting a raw deal—even though no empirical data exists to prove this—explained why whites were now disadvantaged.

As noted above, for the construct of color blindness to work, the dominant culture must lift up some individuals of color who speak the language of color blindness. Some of these black, red, yellow, and brown faces can be lifted up as Supreme Court justices, secretaries of state, or attorneys general because they prove that the white advocates of color blindness are not racist. And as we will see below, the religious face of color blindness insists that because we are all brothers and sisters in Christ, we can learn to tolerate and accept each other. Again, the focus is on the individual and not the social structures. For this reason, color blindness makes reconciliation unattainable: it claims to have achieved basic racial equality in Christ and blames any lingering manifestation of racism on individual bigotry. By contrast, true reconciliation must incorporate a respect for racial and ethnic diversity and advocate a redistribution of global wealth and income through some form of restitution.

THE RELIGIOUS FACE OF EMPIRE

Empires have used racial and ethnic differences to dominate, but they have also used religion. Since the dawn of both empire and religion, the needs and desires of the state, or, better yet, the needs and desires of those privileged by the state, have used faith-based pronouncements to justify their policies. For Christians, the merging of Christianity and empire occurred quite early. In 312 C.E., historians of the time report that Constantine, on the night before the Battle of the Milvian Bridge, dreamed that Christ was instructing him to place his sign (a monogram combining the first letters, X (Greek *chi*) and P (Greek *rho*), off Christ's name) on the soldiers' shields. For the first time, the symbol of Christ, the Prince of Peace, become one with the instruments of death, war, and conquest. By day's end, with the battle won, Constantine attributed victory to the God of the Christians and converted to the faith, although his conversion to Christianity has been viewed as only superficial. In life he served as a high priest to other gods, while among Christians he proclaimed himself the "bishop of bishops." Upon his death he was declared a god by the Senate.

Nevertheless, in 313 C.E., Constantine signed the Edict of Milan, a turning point for Christianity. Until then, Christianity had been the faith of the persecuted and marginalized, but now it became the religion of the emperor. Not surprisingly, the powerful and privileged, and those craving power and privilege, found it advantageous to belong to the emperor's church. It was not long before Christianity became the empire's official religion; however, with worldly recognition came spiritual loss. The relatively simple coming together of Christians for worship prior to Constantine's conversion made way for ornate churches built by the Christians' new benefactor, complete with a form of worship highly influenced by imperial protocol. More disturbing was Constantine's use of the church to advance his imperial policies. The ideology of empire was imposed on the church's theology, depriving believers of its radical pronouncements against the powers and principalities of this world. For example, almost a century after Constantine's conversion, the once-pacifist Christians were developing, thanks to St. Augustine, just war theories—Christian instruction to the empire about waging war.

Constantine's influence on Christianity has continued to this day. As in the times of Rome, Christians of the twenty-first century have their "Constantinian Christians," those who merge the goals of the U.S. empire with the Christian faith, using the latter to justify the former. But Christians are not the only ones who follow a Constantinian model. As Marc Ellis reminds us, there are also Constantinian Muslims and Constantinian Jews, who pursue empire and, on occasion, join each other in this pursuit. It would appear that those who practice empire have more in common with one another than they have with others within their own faith community. Ellis continues:

The danger here is that, in the end, the soul of Judaism, Christianity and Islam that is being fought over has already left the body, if there ever was a body that we can call Judaism, Christianity or Islam. Is it any wonder that we are left with the posers on the right—the ones we love to ridicule like Jerry Falwell, Pat Robertson and Oral Roberts? But we are also left with the likes of Michael Lerner and Arthur Waskow, progressives to be sure, but also brandishing the authoritarian hammer as strongly as their Constantinian counterparts do, which might mean that they are the left wing of Constantinian Judaism. Just as Jim Wallis might be part of the left wing of Constantinian Christianity.[11]

In the final analysis, the Jerry Falwells from the right who call for strengthening the U.S. empire, and the Jim Wallises from the left who call for reforming the U.S. empire, fall short of advocating the dismantling of the empire.

A telling revelation of how Constantinian Christianity has been normalized in American moral thought by its liberal representatives was demonstrated on September 24, 2006, during an angry exchange between former President Bill Clinton and Chris Wallace of Fox News. It was Clinton's anger that drew the attention of the viewing public and the media. What was ignored was one of Clinton's comments concerning the bombing of the USS *Cole* in the port of Aden in 2000. Specifically, Clinton said, "I authorized the CIA to get a crew together to try to kill [Bin Laden]." This, of course, occurred prior to 9/11 when the obvious link between Bin Laden and the 9/11 terrorists attack existed. Still, could a foreign nation discuss the political assassination of a U.S. leader or civilian without consequences? How, then, could the U.S. empire use any moral authority to call for the assassination of foreign political or religious leaders?[12] Should not our response to the *Cole* bombing have been to bring the perpetrators to trial, rather than have the executive branch seek their assassi-

---

[11] Marc H. Ellis, "Are the Ethics of Liberation Theology Still Alive and Relevant? A Jewish Perspective" (paper presented at the annual conference of the Society of Christian Ethics held in January 2007).

[12] U.S. political leaders are not the only ones who call for the assassination of foreign enemies; Christian religious leaders also do, as was the case when televangelist Pat Robertson, on August 22, 2005, called for the assassination of Venezuelan president Hugo Chávez.

nation with no trial? Why do the moral imperatives that reject political assassination apply to other nations but not to the United States? Is this not a characteristic of empire?

Biblical scholar R. S. Sugirtharajah captures the truism of Constantinian Christianity in the opening line of one of his books: "Along with gunboats, opium, slaves and treaties, the Christian Bible became a defining symbol of European expansion" (2001, 1). In many cases, religious messages have been co-opted by the state; in other cases, religion has cooperated with the state. In return for their loyalty, religious leaders have been able to carve out for themselves a sphere of power that allows them to influence the political process. The U.S. empire is no different. In many churches, for example, God and country become synonymous terms as national flags find a space up front in churches and some religious leaders attempt to influence the outcome of elections.

Constantinian Christians reserve for themselves the right to participate in actions, even actions that could be deemed immoral, because of their claim to moral superiority—a moral superiority that they themselves have defined to make a distinction between themselves and the "others": they are terrorists, they cannot be reasoned with; they are inhuman in their actions, therefore, because we are not them, we are civilized, we are rational, we are humane. We may make mistakes, occasionally our judgment may be poor, but our actions will never be perceived as immoral because, after all, we are a "Christian nation."

The formation of a moral dichotomy based on absolute good (us) and absolute evil (them) creates a false reality in which the process of actual moral discernment is trumped by a self-induced delusion of the goodness of the overall character of the United States and its leaders. Those who threaten the dominant culture of empire are dehumanized or demonized before they are dealt with. At times, even asking questions about the global actions of the empire irks our political and religious leaders, who dismiss such discussion as providing comfort to the enemy. In order to preserve "the Good," action, even if perceived as unjust, may need to be undertaken. Ironically, it is in the defense of this *type of* Good that Constantinian Christianity ceases to be Christian.

When a Christian empire is seldom held accountable to the

moral principles of the gospel, Christianity is reduced to personal piety, individual conversion, and philanthropic service, and issues of justice are seldom explored. Few religious leaders or churches question the injustice that can result from neoliberalism or free market economics; few question the values that are produced by such societies. Instead, many religious and political leaders view themselves as God's chosen people, called to witness neoliberal Christianity throughout the world, and this can occur only if the United States remains a militarily and morally strong nation. Strength, then, becomes in itself a religious imperative. Rather than challenging the empire, religious leaders can ignore the military side of empire. Ironically, the religious apologists of the U.S. empire fail to remember that Jesus was also persecuted by the empire of his time; his contemporary religious leaders cried out, "We have no king except Caesar," as they colluded with Rome. History has shown that religious establishments have often been co-opted by states to advance the national interest; today, however, it seems that some leaders supporting the empire have also used their religious positions to support the racist undergirdings of that empire.

Probably the most effective, and most powerful, organization to have successfully sustained the racist face of empire is the Council for National Policy (CNP), formed shortly after the 1980 election of Ronald Reagan. Flushed with victory, a few ultraconservatives had a vision of creating an organization that would implement a right-wing agenda by bringing together the major religious, political, business, and media leaders of the far right. The CNP successfully merged the anti-government, low-tax wing of the Republican party with the religious right. A symbiotic relationship developed between the antigovernment social conservatives representing the elite business community, who would provide the financial funds, and the religious right, who would provide the grassroots organization. The CNP develops strategies to move the country toward the far right but leaves their implementation to the affiliated political and/or religious organizations.[13]

---

[13] The Institute for First Amendment Studies was able to infiltrate the CNP and obtain its 1998 membership list and post it on the Web (Levinson

Before the primaries for the 2000 presidential elections took place, candidate George W. Bush met with the CNP in San Antonio. Locked in a tough primary struggle with John McCain, Bush needed the support of the religious right to win the nomination. Although the session was videotaped, both the Bush administration and the CNP continue to deny requests for full disclosure as to what was discussed at their meeting.[14] Although we do not know what was promised by either side, it is notable that Bush appointed CNP member John Ashcroft as attorney general. Also notable is that shortly after the meeting conservative leaders began to pronounce the younger Bush fit for the mantle of Republican leadership, hence enhancing the CNP's king-making role. By the 2004 presidential election, the CNP had succeeded in bringing out the 2004 vote that gave Bush his first electoral victory. The CNP use of gay-marriage as a wedge issue was highly influential in bringing out the conservative vote, particularly in swing states.[15]

2003, 203). The list reads like a Who's-Who of the religious far right. Cofounders of the CNP were Richard Viguerie (CEO of a fund-raising company with a long-term goal of ending busing to desegregate schools); Paul Weyrich (CNP's first president, and responsible for beginning the Heritage Foundation), and Tim LaHaye (of the popular "Left Behind" apocalyptic novels). The three major financial backers were the Coors family (who made their riches in the brewing industry), the DeVos family (cofounders of the pyramid-scheme company Amway), and the Hunt family (who tried to corner the silver market). Members with religious affiliations include the late Jerry Falwell; strategist Ralph Reed; James Dobson of Focus on the Family; Don Wildmon of the American Family Association; televangelist Pat Robertson; Dr. D. James Kennedy of the influential Coral Ridge Presbyterian Church; Moonie leader Sun Myung Moon; Dr. Paige Patterson, president of Southwestern Baptist Theological Seminary, and Judge Paul Pressler, the two architects of the fundamentalist takeover of the Southern Baptist Convention; and Bob Jones III, head of the university that prohibited interracial dating.

[14] "Bush Administration Reaffirms Ties to Far-Right Council for National Policy," *Church & State* 56, no. 6 (June 1, 2003): 15-16; Albert R. Hunt, "Bush and the Religious Right: Conviction or Convenience?" *Wall Street Journal*, July 6, 2000; Jim Yardley, "The 2000 Campaign" *New York Times*, May 19, 2000.

[15] David D. Kirkpatrick, "Club of the Most Powerful," *New York Times*, August 28, 2004.

The CNP proposes a theocracy that assumes its own correctness—a correctness that leads to a worldview and a world mission. Influenced by the historical residue of Manifest Destiny, the religious right sees itself called on to save the world. No doubt, my previous Sunday School teacher's rendition of the Book of Jonah would resonate with most CNP members. Blessed by God to be part of a democratic nation, they understand that to whom much is given, much is expected. They are expected to spread their Christian values and system of democracy to all the nations of the world, by force if necessary. Domestically, they stand in the gap between an angry God and a nation that has turned to secularism: they have the responsibility to restore family values—to outlaw abortions, restore school prayer, quash homosexual rights legislation, advocate abstinence as the chosen form of sex education, and remove "activist" judges. Ironically, while many CNP members claim to be "born-again" Christians wishing to influence public policy away from secular humanism, in actuality, their agenda seems less influenced by the gospel message than by capitalism and a nativist ideology. In effect, the CNP protects white privilege and prevents reconciliation across racial and ethnic divides, although black professionals with conservative credentials who support a conservative agenda are welcomed and even provided membership (in limited numbers, of course), but, not surprisingly, those who belong to lower economic classes are excluded.[16]

An example of the color blindness advocated by the CNP can be found in the activities of Promise Keepers, an organization for Christian men supported by CNP members like Pat Robertson, the late Jerry Falwell, D. James Kennedy, and James Dobson, who supply money, speakers, writers, and advertising. The strategy of Promise Keepers is to bring about racial reconciliation by confessing one's sins related to racism, accepting forgiveness, and supplying mutual support to men attempting to live godly lives. Reconciliation is often reduced to participating in multiracial worship services. While such symbolic acts may eventually be

---

[16] Marc Ambinder, "Inside the Council for National Policy," *ABC News*, May 2, 2001.

beneficial, they do not necessarily foster structural changes. Missing from this formula is any attempt to combat institutionalized racism through education, political activism, or the use of corporate pressure. In fact, such tactics are discouraged (Alumkal 2004, 202-3).

As Antony W. Alumkal points out,

> Defining racism as a spiritual problem that is immune to secular solutions gives whites license to oppose affirmative action, welfare, and other divisive government programs. Furthermore, whites who are nostalgic for a sense of ethnic attachment can treat evangelical Christianity as a quasi-ethnic identity, a move that is encouraged by evangelicals' sense of themselves as an embattled religious minority in the contemporary United States. Finally, whites can respond to their history as "oppressors" by catharic acts of repentance, as well as by assertions that Christian identity transcends race, while fully retaining the fruits of white privilege. (Alumkal 2004, 205)

Unfortunately, this approach can lead to the absurd. During a 1996 Promise Keepers gathering of forty-five thousand men in Atlanta, a Native American told the crowd: "We forgive the white man for taking our land and our buffalo because if you had not come, we would not know about Jesus Christ."[17]

By stressing individual actions instead of efforts to change the social structures, those who are privileged by those same structures feel righteous for having apologized for past racist acts. Meanwhile, they continue to benefit from the status quo. Winant concludes his observations by claiming that

> the biological racism of the far right, the expedient and subtextual racism of the new right, and the bad-faith antiracism of the neoconservatives have many differences from each other, but they have at least one thing in common. They all

---

[17] Norm R. Allen, "The Religious Right," *Free Inquiry* 20, no. 4 (Fall 2000): 38.

seek to maintain the long-standing associations between whiteness and U.S. political traditions, between whiteness and U.S. nationalism, between whiteness and universalism (2004, 66).

THE GOD OF EMPIRE/THE GOD OF THE GOSPEL

Contrary to the sentiments expressed by the Native American mentioned above who addressed the 1996 Atlanta gathering of the Promise Keepers, Tink Tinker, a Native American religious scholar, describes how the Christian message was proclaimed to his people:

> It is curious that Christians are led logically to believe that "God," until the birth of Jesus, cared only for one small people on the face of the earth, leaving all others to ignorance, "sin," idolatry, self-destruction, and eternal damnation. For Indian peoples the message only becomes more difficult. It is conveyed through the clear inference that "God's" love (in the Jesus event) was denied Indian peoples until God, in God's graciousness, sent White people to kill us, lie to us, steal our land, and proclaim the saving gospel to us. (2004, 236)

If we begin with the assumption that the basic mission of Jesus is to bring life, as expressed in his own words: "I came that they may have life, and have it abundantly" (John 10:10), and if we affirm that the mission of the Evil One is to bring death and destruction—"Your adversary the devil is prowling around like a roaring lion seeking someone to devour" (1 Pet. 5:8)—then we can conclude that those acts that bring about life are of God, while those acts that bring about death are not. The god of the Assyrian empire, Assur, craved supremacy over every other deity and nation in the region. To achieve this goal, the Assyrians conquered their neighbors, bringing death and destruction to them in the name of their god. Because Assur was a god who offered death abundantly, Assur was a satanic god. In similar fashion, the god of the U.S. empire, as manifested in Jesus Christ, brings death and destruction to much of the world's disenfranchised. Do these defenders of empire truly worship the Jesus of the gospel message? We must consistently test the Spirit that claims to be of God, because gods of empires have proven themselves to be "like roaring lions seeking the marginalized to devour." Mahatma Gandhi understood this well. In a 1918 speech on India's civilization he observed that the European empire was satanic because it produced death (2004, 102). Such satanic gods of empire must die once and for all.

The continuation of oppressive structures abroad and at home forces those who suffer because of their race or ethnicity to wonder about the very character of a God who appears silent in the face of injustice as many continue to be sacrificed so that others can maintain their power and privilege. If those on the margins are able to determine who is this God that appears to turn God's gaze away from the suffering of God's people, then they, as well as those from the dominant culture choosing to stand in solidarity with them, can determine what actions are required so that this silent God can finally be heard.

The Christians of the first century were accused of atheism and thrown to the lions because they rejected the god of the dominant culture of their time. Before we can begin any process of reconciliation, we need more of those kinds of "atheists"—persons willing to lose their lives or livelihoods because they refuse to believe in the god of today's powers and principalities. The gods that have historically sided with the powerful, the oppressors, the colonial powers, must die, even the god that blesses only America. All idols that bestow privilege on people based on their race or ethnicity must die along with the Christendom they represent. Only then can we hope for the birth of the church.

Black ethicist Delores Williams reminds us:

> To be a Christian in North America is to wage war against the white culture, social and religious values that make the genocide of black people [and I would add all marginalized people] possible. To be a Christian is to wage this war in the name of Jesus and his ministerial vision of relationship,

which involved whipping the money changers (read those in charge of genocidal values) out of the Temple. (1993, 201)

Can those who are oppressed reconcile with forces that produce death? Forces that are satanic? Forces incarnated as empire? No. Reconciliation requires putting away the false idols of privilege and power. Reconciliation occurs apart from empire, not with empire. Those who are privileged must join in solidarity with those residing on the underside if any hope of reconciliation is to exist. Reconciliation cannot take place until the God of the oppressed, the God incarnated in the lives and suffering of today's crucified people, the God that demands justice, be allowed to reign.

3

Reflecting on Jonah

WHEN WE HEAR OF JONAH, we think immediately of his
adventures with the whale, and our interest often begins and ends
there. Seldom do Christians recall that the story of Jonah is a
story of reconciliation. In the Jewish tradition, the story of Jonah
and reconciliation play highly significant roles that are generally
ignored or forgotten by Christians. The ten-day period starting
with Rosh Hashanah and ending with Yom Kippur (the Day of
Atonement) is known as Yamim Noraim (the Days of Awe) or
the Days of Repentance. During these High Holy Days of the
Jewish calendar, every Jewish believer spends time undertaking
serious introspection to consider the sins of the previous year and
repent of them. Believers can atone only for sins that exist
between them and their God, not for sins committed against
other persons. To atone for those transgressions, a believer must
first seek to reconcile with the offended person by correcting the
wrong.

During the afternoon service on the Day of Atonement, the
Book of Jonah is read as *haftarah* (reading from the prophets),
signaling that God prefers to redeem rather than to punish. The
central theme of Jonah is clearly repentance. But who is being
called to repent? The Assyrians of Nineveh, or Jonah, or both
parties? It is the prophet Jonah who is appointed to be God's messenger to bring God's call for repentance to Nineveh.[1] This may

---

[1] The Hebrew name Jonah, *yônâ* literally means "dove," which is not
only a metaphor for Israel (Hos. 7:11;11:11; Ps 74:19) and a symbol of the

seem an odd choice, as Jonah, an Israelite, is among those abused and oppressed by the Assyrian empire. It is not surprising that Jonah does not welcome this assignment; he would undoubtedly prefer that God rain down fire and brimstone upon the heads of all those who oppress others and who continue to benefit from the oppressive social structures of empire. However, Jonah is also responsible before God. As the Gospel of Matthew points out, sin is not only the outward action committed by the individual but also the internal emotions and thoughts (Matt. 5:21-28). Jonah, who wishes the destruction of the Ninevites, is also at fault.

This, then, is the dilemma faced by those who take the Book of Jonah seriously. The message of Jonah is one of redemption for *both* the oppressor and the oppressed. Even though redemption of the oppressor can lead to the destruction of the oppressed, both are subject to God's mercy and God's grace. This is a difficult message. Does faithfulness to the biblical text mean further oppression for those on the margins, whether of the Assyrian empire or the U.S. empire? Does repentance on the part of the dominant culture mean that those on the margins are simply to "forgive and forget?" What is the Christian duty of the injured party? What principles can Christians follow to bring about reconciliation?

CONSTRUCTING GOD

Jonah truly believed that God was on his side. Jonah's mistake, however, was the same one that is made by many religious people today. He projected his biases and prejudices onto God, assuming that God would execrate and renounce those whom Jonah execrated and renounced, and that God's doctrines and

---

Holy Spirit for Christians (Matt. 3:16), but also a universal signifier of peace and reconciliation. For Jewish and Christian practitioners, the symbolic meaning of the dove is rooted in the story of Noah, which records the dove bringing the patriarch a branch from an olive tree as a sign that the deluge of God's wrath has come to an end, opening the way to reconciliation (Gen. 8:10-11).

beliefs would correspond to his own. And while a preferential option did exist for Jonah, as it does for the oppressed and poor everywhere, Jonah should not have allowed the prejudices that informed him, regardless of how justified they may have been, to fuse or be confused with God's understanding of and hopes for the Assyrians. As wicked as an empire may be, God does not rejoice in the destruction and death of those privileged by it. To project Jonah's prejudices upon the Almighty is to forget that the Book of Jonah is to tell us about God, who speaks both first and last in the story, and not just about Jonah.

Still, the Book of Jonah reveals for us what the prophet perceives to be a major flaw in God's character—God is unjust. To forgive an oppressor appears contrary to any sense of justice. This theme is taken up by the psalmist, who also struggles with a God who seems silent as evildoers continue to enrich themselves. According to the psalmist:

> I was envious of the arrogant, and looked upon the peace of the wicked. For them, there are no pangs to their death, their bodies are fat. They do not toil as others do, no human afflictions for them! So pride enchains them, violence the garment that covers them. Their spite oozes like fat, their hearts drip with slyness. They scoff and speak in cruel malice, lofty advocates of force. They set their mouths against Heaven and their tongues can dictate on earth. This is why my people turn to them and the waters of a full cup are drained, asking, "How will God know? Does the Most High know everything? Behold: these are the wicked, at ease and getting richer!" Surely, why should I keep my heart pure, and wash my hands in innocence, if you plague me all day long and discipline me every morning? (Ps. 73:3-14)

The psalmist not only articulates Jonah's dilemma but also reveals the doubt that lurks in the hearts of marginalized communities of color today. Why are oppressors not punished? Why do they grow richer and more prestigious? How can justice exist if they die in peace in the comfort of their satin-sheeted beds while others die in hovels? Those who are supposed to be God's chosen people, for whom God makes a preferential option, are susceptible because of their disenfranchisement to more illnesses, fewer opportunities for education and employment, and shorter life spans. Where is cosmic justice to be found? And adding salt to the wounds of marginality, God calls the oppressed to reach out to their tormentors so that they too can be saved? How can we not conclude that God is indeed unjust?

Perhaps the problem lies in how we are defining justice. Does justice mean revenge? Melanie Bash, a clinical psychologist, and Anthony Bash, a New Testament scholar, remind us that the aim of a therapist is to help the client through a voluntary and unilateral act of the will to let go of the past, experience inner healing, and move toward fulfillment. If we recognize that the New Testament distinguishes between forgiveness and reconciliation,[2] then we can begin to understand that forgiveness benefits those who have been the victims. A subsequent and separate process of reconciliation then demands addressing the injustices that allowed the oppressor to grow richer and more powerful (Bash and Bash 2004, 43). Still, how does one let go of the past if it involves the death of one's child or community, either immediately at the hands of the Assyrian empire of old, or slowly through the economic strangulation of today's neoliberal economic system? Can a person truly let go without internalizing the pain?

Perhaps the first party the oppressed need to forgive is God— for refusing to punish the oppressor. Our first response, then, even before dealing with the oppressor, might be to cry out to God in anger and, yes, maybe even hatred, for allowing *this* to happen to us. If we vent our anger toward God, we may find ourselves in good company. Recall Moses, who shook his fist at God crying out "Why have you done evil to your servant? And why have I not found grace in your sight?" (Num. 11:11). Even Jesus, while dying on the cross, cried out in anguish from the midst of his abandonment and desertion to a silent deity, "My God, my

---

[2] The father, in the parable of the Prodigal Son (Luke 15:11-32) forgave his wayward child prior to his return. This is forgiveness. Reconciliation takes place when the son acknowledges and repents from his wrongdoing and makes a move to rectify the existing estrangement.

God, why did you forsake me?" (Matt. 27:46). It is good to come honestly before God, as did Moses and Jesus, and express our sense of frustration, helplessness, and even anger to a God who appears to be absent. Crying out, "I hate you, God, because of what you have allowed to happen to me and my people" may be a first step in learning how to forgive. God is neither afraid of, nor intimidated by, our outbursts. Nor is God waiting and ready to punish us for expressing the true feelings in our hearts. Denying feelings of abandonment by a God in whom we placed our total faith is destructive to our spiritual and physical health. A healthier approach is to wrestle with God, as did Jacob (Gen. 32:23-33), until God finally deals with our situation and offers a blessing—even if we end up limping away.

God Does as God Pleases

Whether we like it or not, God does as God pleases. In the words of the psalmist: "But our God is in heaven: God has done whatever was pleasing to Godself" (Ps. 115:3). Does this mean that God is as capricious as the Greek and Roman gods of old? No. If we claim that God is love, and that God's love is manifested as justice, then God's actions must be based on just principles. How God defines and manifests love and justice will differ from one particular social location to another as they are informed by different cultures, traditions, and historical periods. Does this mean that justice is only a social construction whose definition differs among different times and peoples, as postmodernists might claim, or that one "Truth" of what justice is can never exist? Yes and no. The answer is yes, in that we all construct our own definitions and understandings of justice and then use those definitions to judge our world and define our God. But are those definitions "Truth?" Not necessarily. Because our particular social location influences how we see and define the world, all truth proclamations must be suspect. This is what liberation theologians call the hermeneutic of suspicion. While the biblical texts may provide principles that can assist us in understanding God's sense of justice, we—because of our finite minds—always risk falling short of the mark.

Although we may not be able fully to capture Truth because we lack God's mind, we can arrive at truths that describe the justice of God with the guidance of biblical texts, even though those texts do not always agree. Rabbinic writing tells us:

> They asked Wisdom, "What is the sinner's punishment?" It told them: "Sinners—let them be pursued by [their] evil" [Prov. 12:31]. They asked Prophecy, "What is the sinner's punishment?" It told them: "The soul that sins—it shall die!" [Ezek. 18:20]. They asked Torah, "What is the sinner's punishment?" It told them: "Let him bring a guilt-offering and gain atonement!" They asked the Holy One, Blessed be He, "What is the sinner's punishment?" He told them: "Let him repent and gain atonement!"[3]

God wishes all, including the most vile of oppressors, to find redemption. The prophet Jeremiah records God as saying, "The instant I speak about uprooting a nation or a kingdom, and smashing it and causing it to perish; if that nation of which I have spoken turns away from its evil, I will repent of the evil that I thought to do to them" (Jer. 18:7-8). Yes—God will punish the wickedness of classism, racism, and sexism, but God can offer forgiveness instead of retribution if the oppressor chooses to "turn away from its evil." God's actions are not limited.

It is important to note that the instrument that God chooses to warn oppressors of what awaits them—if not in this life, then the next--may be the suffering of those experiencing the evil generated by an oppressor. Indeed, it is the stone rejected that becomes the cornerstone of God's construction (Ps. 118:32). The task of the prophets, those chosen by God and the ones for whom God makes a preferential option, is to proclaim God's message of repentance.

God Loves the Oppressors

A pivotal story for many suffering people in the world has been the story of the exodus. This is the story of a God who

---

[3] Midrash, Yerushalmi Makkos (Jerusalem Talmud, *Makkot* 2:6).

enters history and personally leads God's people away from the tyranny and slavery of Egypt toward liberation in the promised land. This hope that God eventually hears the cry of the oppressed and acts to bring about their liberation resonates powerfully with oppressed groups.[4] As the story goes, at one point the children of Israel are trapped between the Sea of Reeds and the advancing armies of the Egyptians. In a dramatic intervention, God splits the sea in two and the former slaves walk to safety across dry ground. Then when Pharaoh's chariots pursue the fleeing Hebrews, the waters close in, drowning the enemies of God's chosen people (Exod. 14). Miriam, the sister of Moses, picks up a timbrel and sings praises to the Lord: "Sing to YHWH for surely God has triumphed; the horse and its rider God has thrown into the sea" (Exod. 15:20-21). God has made a preferential option for the slaves by destroying the oppressors of the Egyptian empire. Liberation of the oppressed causes the death of the oppressors.

Jewish tradition can prove helpful for Christians trying to understand God's feelings toward the oppressors. For example, "Harav David Feinstein points out that God's compassion extends to all His creatures. As God said in silencing the angels who wished to sing His praises after the Egyptians drowned in the Sea of Reeds: 'My handiwork is drowning in the sea and you presume to sing praise?'" (Scherman 1978, 141). Oppressors, like the oppressed, are created in the image of God: because they also contain the *imago Dei*, their lives, no matter how deprived, have sanctity. Hope exists, even for reprobates like the apostle Saul, who was committed to the death and destruction of Christians (Acts 9:1-2). While death may be brought about by their own hardened hearts (if not in this world, then eternally), their demise is to be pitied, not celebrated. God does not desire death of either body or soul, even for oppressors. The prophet Jeremiah reminds us that God has said, "For I will forgive their iniquity and will remember their sins no more" (31:34). These words are echoed

---

[4] An exception is found among Native Americans, who see themselves instead as the Canaanites, those who have been made homeless by the chosen people.

by the prophet Micah: "Who is a God like you, who forgives iniquity and passes by the transgression of the remnant of his inheritance? God does not stay angry forever but delights in showing mercy. God will return to show us compassion; God will trample our iniquities and hurl all our sins into the depths of the sea" (Mic. 7:18-19).

We can paraphrase language from the Gospel of John, "For God so loved Nineveh that God sent his beloved prophet Jonah, that whosoever believes in his message shall not perish but have life." The meaning of the biblical text is clear: God loves all created beings, including oppressors, and wants them to repent and regain their humanity. While many falsely accept their comfortable lifestyle as God's blessings, the fruits of hard work, or an entitlement due to their overall superiority, those who oppress others, in fact, forfeit part of their humanity through their complicity with oppressive structures. The benefits obtained through power and privilege lead many to turn a blind eye to the plight of the marginalized and a deaf ear to their cries for justice.

Oppressive structures create an inhuman existence for both the disenfranchised and the dominant culture. Repentance, forgiveness, and reconciliation form the steps in the process of reclaiming one's humanity and dignity, for both the oppressed and for those who benefit from their oppression. The Christian God that has been historically professed is a God who does not want to see anyone lost. This God will leave ninety-nine sheep in a field to find the one lost lamb (Luke 15:4-7). Any serious Christian discourse on reconciliation must incorporate a God who loves even oppressors and desires to bring them back into the fold. It seems at times that God is more concerned with the redemption of the spiritually lost than with inflicting revenge or enforcing a strict understanding of justice. According to the prophet Ezekiel:

> But if the wicked turn away from all sins committed and keep all my statutes and do justice and righteousness, surely shall they live; they shall not die. All transgressions done shall not be mentioned. Because of the just things done, they shall live. Do I actually desire the death of the wicked?

declares the Lord YHWH. Rather, am I not pleased when
they turn from their ways and live? . . . Yet the house of
Israel says, "The way of the Lord is not just." Are my ways
fair, O house of Israel? Is it not your ways that are not fair?
. . . I take no pleasure in the death of anyone, declares the
Lord YHWH. Repent and live!" (18:21-23, 29, 32)

However, claiming God's care and love for the oppressor
should never be an excuse to ignore or exclude the requirements
of social, political, and economic justice. Yes, God loves the
oppressor, but God's love is strong enough to *demand* the oppressor's repentance and rejection of oppressive structures. It is a love
that leads the offender toward justice. As the Gospel of Matthew
points out, on that last day, when the heavens are opened and the
Son of God sits upon the throne of judgment, the people will be
divided as are sheep and goats, judged by how they interacted
with "the least among us" (Matt. 25:31-46). Salvation is not
determined by which church you have joined, what charities you
support, what profession of faith you voice, or which doctrines
you uphold. It is not our actions of feeding the hungry, clothing
the naked, taking in the alien, or visiting the ill and incarcerated
that bring about our salvation. Salvation remains a free gift
offered because of God's love. Jesus, however, linked our response
to the marginalized as the outward manifestation of an inward
conversion. To ignore the marginalized is to reject God. As the
Proverbs remind us, "Those who oppress the poor curse their
Maker; but the one who has mercy on the needy gives God
honor" (14:31). How, then, do Christians reconcile God's love
for both oppressor and oppressed with God's demand for justice?
Is it really possible?

CONSTRUCTING SCAPEGOATS

The demands of our Christian faith raise many other important questions that are closely related to the need for reconciliation. In the first place, how can self-professed Christian rulers
steal, rape, or kill people from other lands? Don't the fundamen-

tals of Christianity clash with the prerequisites of empire building? In the history of the United States, how could Christians have justified the genocide of Amerindians, or the enslavement of Africans, the internment of Asians, or the pauperization of Hispanics? How did the American builders of empire reconcile their oppressive actions with the gospel message of love and liberation?

In the past, colonialists were convinced—or convinced themselves—that the violence they unleashed and the misery they caused were justified and, in fact, necessary for the good of all. They perceived the to-be-conquered or those already conquered as either nonhuman or at a lower stage on the evolutionary scale. Through a *false consciousness* created by the imagination of civilized Europeans, the indigenous people of the Americas, Africa, and Asia were seen as backward and primitive and in need of Christian tutelage. It was the burden and mission of superior Eurocentric Christians to bring their light into the darkness of the "Other," paternalistically leading the less developed to civilization. (Today the language of neoliberalism may use the term democracy in place of civilization.) In exchange for their supposed cultural advancement in the here and now, and hope for salvation in the hereafter, those perceived as inferior (in other words, nonwhites) contributed their resources to enrich the center, usually at the expense of their own underdevelopment. This illusion held true whether the "uncivilized" resided on foreign soil or within the empire. The effects of more than five centuries of "civilizing" and "Christianizing" native peoples still exist today for those living in Africa, Asia, and Latin America and for their descendants residing within the empire.

The Christian builders of empire had to justify what otherwise would have been the blatant imposition of oppressive structures to accumulate wealth and power for themselves. To do this, they constructed a social order that appeared not only normative but also possessed of a spirituality. Instead of remaining the faith of the "least of these," Christianity had to be reconstructed to justify un-Christian acts. It was not enough to construct the marginalized of the world as inferior and thus responsible for their menial existence, they must also be blamed for the misfortune that befell them as punishment by or disfavor before God. In effect, they become the necessary scapegoats offered up for the sins of empire building.

The concept of scapegoating is central to many biblical texts. Leviticus 16, for example, laid out the rituals concerning Yom Kippur, the Day of Atonement. As noted earlier in this chapter, Yom Kippur, the most important Jewish holy day, is a solemn day of fasting when God's people search their hearts and seek reconciliation with God and neighbor. Leviticus instructs believers to purify their temple and then to sacrifice a goat to atone for the sins and impurities they committed against God throughout the year. The Babylonian Talmud, in citing Leviticus 17:11, notes that there can be no atonement without blood,[5] a concept repeated in the New Testament (Heb. 9:22). A biblical concept is thus established that blood must be shed for forgiveness and reconciliation to occur.

In the temple ritual of Yom Kippur, a second goat was then presented to the priest, who placed his hands on the goat's head. The Hebrew word used for this second goat has traditionally been understood as "the goat that escapes"—thus the original concept of the *scapegoat*. The priest symbolically placed upon the scapegoat the sins of the community. Then the goat was driven to the wilderness, where it was released, carrying with it the sins of the people.[6]

René Girard, an influential French philosopher, has explored the function of scapegoating in crises that remind humans of their mortality, such as a political disturbance, famine, or plague. Such monumental upheavals cause the collapse of the "social order evidenced by the disappearance of rules and 'differences' that define cultural divisions" (1986, 12). Girard argues that human society unites during times of crises to combat such crises through what he terms a "victimage mechanism" (1987, 23-30). This happens when the persecutors "convince themselves that a small number of people, or even a single individual, despite relative weakness, is extremely harmful to the whole of society" (1986,

---

[5] Babylonian Talmud, *Yoma* 5a and *Zevahim* 6a.

[6] It is interesting to note that the sin-laden goat is not offered to Yahweh, the Hebrew God, but rather to the demonic figure Azazel, the goat-god (Lev. 16:26).

15). Jews, for example, became the scapegoats during the plague of the fourteenth century. Likewise, African Americans were lynched during the nineteenth and twentieth centuries as scapegoats for poor whites who blamed their economic situation on the menace of black competition in the marketplace. Today, marginalized communities still serve as the scapegoats for crime, white underemployment, or low income levels and are transformed into the cause of such crises. Their deaths, figuratively and literally, thus have the potential to produce greater peace, security, and tranquility for the society at large.

Unfortunately for the marginalized, destruction of the scapegoats simultaneously preserves and disguises the injustice visited upon them. During cultural upheavals, those calling for the sacrifice of scapegoats are usually ignorant of the true causes of the crises they face, but they find strength and reassurance in numbers. The result is often mob violence that collectively persecutes victims in order to eliminate the perceived cause of a crisis (Girard 1986, 12-15). In the worst case, blood is actually shed to bring unity and reconciliation among the perpetrators.

The belief that the victim's death can reestablish community unity and solidarity is a false myth that masks the obvious—that the innocent were murdered by the dominant culture in order to preserve their privileged position. Girard makes the point that while Jesus's passion story is structurally identical to murder through the mechanism of scapegoating, it effectively debunks the myth (1987, 154-70). Jesus's crucifixion ceases to be explained as a necessary price demanded by an angry god who requires satisfaction. Instead, the passion story tells of an innocent man hoping to foster reconciliation among oppressors. Or, as Caiaphas, the high priest at the time, prophetically said, "Do you not know that it is profitable for us that one man die for the people, rather than for all the nation to perish?" (John 11:50). In the end, the gospel records that reconciliation did indeed take place: although Pilate (the Roman occupier) and Herod (the local elite) "had previously been enemies, they were reconciled [on the day of Jesus's crucifixion]" (Luke 23:12). Girard does not spiritualize the death of Jesus on the cross. Instead, it is the account of Jesus dying as a scapegoat to preserve the unity between Rome and the elite in Jerusalem. And, like him, those today who are crucified as scapegoats are sacrificed to preserve reconciliation within different elements of the dominant culture.

Girard's analysis rings true in explaining mob violence, but it can also be applied to the everyday, uneventful social order within an empire. Scapegoats are not just for times of crisis; they are also needed in times of peace and prosperity when they can be used to divert attention from the injustices experienced by people of color and their fellow whites who are economically disenfranchised. Although whiteness does provide greater access and opportunity when compared to people of color, it is not enough to reach the exalted status of the elite few who fully benefit from how society is structured within empire. Many whites who experience disenfranchisement have the same desires as elite Euroamericans, specifically, the desire for power and privilege as demonstrated through their interaction with marginalized groups of color. Girard terms this desire for a different status "mimetic" (imitation) desire.

Unfortunately, such mimetic desire can lead to social conflict. Instead of waiting for conflict to erupt, sacrifices are occasionally offered to cover the sins of oppression and mask the causes of potential conflict, such as the present unequal distribution of wealth. It is not surprising that grievances existing between the elite and their economically disenfranchised compatriots, if left unattended, can ignite into communitywide crises. Today, the offering of scapegoats, more often in the form of people of color, during times of tranquility preserves the solidarity of the overall dominant culture. Sacrificing those on the margins becomes a preventive measure. How else can an assembly worker of twenty years make sense of being laid off because of corporate downsizing? Or how can a moderately above average high school student explain her rejection to an Ivy League college? Or how can a couple with decent jobs understand why their combined income is insufficient for groceries or the rent?

Scapegoating of the marginalized not only brings about reconciliation among the members of the dominant class, it also provides poor and disenfranchised Euroamericans with an explanation for their own economic deprivation. They do not often blame the elite or fellow whites within the dominant culture who might be responsible for their low wages or lack of job security; rather, they blame those who are incorrectly perceived as benefiting from welfare, affirmative action, or government handouts. For example, it is those "illegal" aliens who are taking away our jobs and benefiting from our social services. Instead of holding those above with positions of power liable, blame rolls downward to people of color, whose function now becomes preserving Euroamerican unity.

It is important to note that sacrificing the scapegoat not only provides unity; it also nullifies any role the victim may have as truth-bearer. Girard points out that it is the victim who can reveal "the truth of the system, its relativity, its fragility, and its mortality" (1986, 21). Why? Because victims of oppression have a better understanding of the causes of their disenfranchisement and how their oppressors benefit from the prevailing structures. This epistemological privilege makes the prophets, like Jonah, important messengers to empires.

Another important factor to consider is the fate of those marginalized people who have achieved success despite the dominant culture. Their success disproves the myth of their inferiority constructed by the dominant culture. Because a successful Asian businesswoman, a brilliant African American scholar, an insightful Amerindian author all threaten the constructed reality of the dominant culture, their success is explained as a result of unfair advantages. I recall a colleague of my wife at a previous institution expressing gladness for affirmative action because he was able to work with her—a person of color. Success of the marginalized disproves the dominant culture's constructed reality and must either be explained away or silenced.

Offering up scapegoats also allows those in power to eliminate potential "troublemakers" and "outside agitators." Those who openly and aggressively challenge Eurocentric supremacy can easily find themselves in precarious situations. While their death is always an option (for example, the systematic murder of Black Panther leaders toward the end of the last century), silencing can also take place through the loss of employment or roadblocks to advancement. Societal structures that effectively silence potential opponents are powerful instruments for maintaining the status quo of marginalized groups. Employees abused at their places of work often remain silent for fear of losing their jobs. In most cases, feeding one's family trumps any call for justice. Finally, those from the disenfranchised class who have been able to succeed in spite of unfair social structures become potential competitors for economic, social, and political power. Here, then, is the crux of our struggle with the concept of reconciliation. Scapegoating attempts to undermine the achievements of the marginalized so as to advantage those with Eurocentric privilege. This is why reconciliation becomes difficult. How can scapegoats reconcile with those who are offering them up for sacrifices?

RETHINKING CHRIST'S SACRIFICE

Was Jesus the ultimate scapegoat? Why did his blood need to be spilled? Although Christian theologians have historically wrestled with these questions, the early church did not. Its focus was more on understanding the nature of Jesus the Christ and the concept of the Trinity. Origen (185-254?) considered Jesus's death as a ransom to be paid to the devil, and Athanasius (328-373) viewed Christ as our representative. It was Anselm of Canterbury (1033-1109) who first developed a carefully reasoned doctrine of atonement in *Cur Deus Homo*. Anselm reasoned that the death of Jesus was necessary to satisfy God's anger. Because humans were sinful, they could not perform the work of atonement, but satisfaction for sin must be made nonetheless. Only God could initiate the atonement process, and only a sinless God-as-human-being could complete the process, make restitution, and restore creation. Abelard (1079-1142), a younger contemporary of Anselm, insisted instead that Jesus's death demonstrated God's exemplary love, which is the basis for forgiveness and reconciliation, and humans would respond. Martin Luther (1483-1546) adapted this "satisfaction theory" of Anselm by emphasizing that Jesus's death was a voluntary sacrifice by him on our behalf. This understanding, called "justification by faith," was foundational in Reformation thinking (Aulén 1969, 1-4).[7]

Generally speaking, Eurocentric theologies have incorporated the concept of Jesus's death as a form of ransom for humanity. We are the ones who should have been condemned for our sins, but Jesus died instead. His blood cleanses us. Our salvation, understood as everlasting life in the hereafter, is contingent solely upon accepting this free gift paid for by Jesus. Only Jesus could have satisfied the debt owed, and we can accept Jesus as Lord and Savior in gratitude.

Some theologians today, however, maintain that this interpretation of atonement is problematic and may, in fact, impede reconciliation. They question the belief that because Jesus paid the ransom by his death so that others might live, suffering and death become salvific. This is particularly true because often the outcome of such a belief is that those hoping to imitate Jesus are taught to accept abuse, pain, humiliation, and violation as "carrying their cross." An example of this way of thinking can be found in the Methodist church primer of 1852 known as "Capers's Catechism," which was approved by the Methodist General Conference and used throughout the antebellum South. Slaves were taught that their servitude to whites was God's will and God's call for their lives (Hoyt 1991, 27-28). Their suffering in the here and now would be offset by the promise of heavenly glory.

But how can the suffering of the just be redemptive? Forgotten is the understanding that injustice and unjust suffering are first and foremost sin. And if this sin is not acknowledged, reconciliation cannot take place. What, then, was redemptive about Jesus's crucifixion? It was not the concept of sacrificial substitution (Jesus as the ultimate sacrifice was killed for our sins). Rather, Jesus's life, death, and resurrection became redemptive in his praxis of accompanying the disenfranchised of his time—a solidarity demonstrated even unto death.

---

[7] In 1999, the Joint Declaration on the Doctrine of Justification, a document created by and agreed to by clerical representatives of the Lutheran World Federation, representing Lutherans worldwide, and the Catholic Church, apparently resolved the conflict over "justification by faith" that was partly responsible for the Protestant Reformation.

Nevertheless, the thinking that created the concept of sacrificial substitution is not limited to the crucifixion of Jesus. Today, for example, the forced globalization of the world economy demands sacrificial victims, most of whom are the world's poor, primarily people of color. With capital the god that is worshiped, those on the economic periphery die while producing riches so that the center of power can participate in all the comfort that life has to offer. To a great extent, the wealth, power, and might of the few literally create suffering and death for the many. In other words, it can be said that the death of those perceived to be inferior is the sacrifice offered as ransom so that the few can enjoy their excess. Like Jesus, the marginalized of the earth die so that those with power and privilege can have life abundantly.

But scripture teaches that Jesus understands the plight of today's crucified people, who hang on crosses dedicated to the idols of race, class, gender, and heterosexual superiority, not because he is with them (although he is) but, more important, because he is one of them. "Insofar as you have done this to the least of these, *you did it to me*" (Matt. 25:40). More important than any theology that reduces the crucifixion to a doctrine of substitution (I should have been crucified, but instead Jesus took my place), is the understanding that the crucifixion of Jesus is God's solidarity with the countless multitudes of history and with those who continue to be crucified today. Jesus's death on the cross should never be reduced to a sacrifice needed to pacify a God offended by human sin.

Ignored for centuries by Eurocentric Christian theology was that Jesus, as fully human, was put to death, like so many others then and now, by civil and religious leaders who saw him as a threat to their power. Jesus was a victim of empire. The importance of the cross for the world's marginalized is that they have a God who understands their trials and tribulations because Jesus, God-in-the-flesh, also suffered trials and tribulations. The good news is not so much that Jesus was crucified, but that Jesus rose from the dead, not to show off God's power but to provide hope for the crucified of every time and place that they too will be ultimately victorious over the oppression they face.

Forgetting that the cross is a symbol of evil allows for the easy romanticization of those who are marginalized as some sort of hyper-Christians for the "cross" they carry. Such views tend to honor their suffering, encouraging a form of quietism where suffering is stoically borne, rather than encouraging actions to end unnecessary or unjust suffering. If salvation exists in Jesus Christ's life and resurrection as well as in his death, then the crucifixion can be seen for what it was—the unjust murder of a just man by the dominant culture of his time. The crucifixion becomes Jesus Christ's act of solidarity with those relegated to the underside. It offers reassurance to the disenfranchised that Christ understands their sufferings and the hope that victory will be theirs.

It is important to remember that while the crucifixion signifies Jesus's solidarity with the oppressed, the cross does not benefit only the marginalized. Those complicit with oppressive structures can also find solidarity in the passion of Jesus. Hope for salvation on the part of the dominant culture is contingent upon their crucifying their power and privilege on the cross. Only by dying to their complicity with oppression and seeking to live a life that pursues justice can one find a new life in Christ. In the words of James Cone, "Reconciliation means *death* and only those who are prepared to die in the struggle for freedom will experience new life with God" (1975, 239).

Constructing Reconciliation

As Jonah awaited the outcome of his message, he climbed a hill overseeing Nineveh so as better to witness God's destruction of that wicked city. Jonah knew that the very survival of his own people was at stake. If God showed mercy to Israel's archenemy, the Assyrian empire, Jonah's own people would eventually face destruction at Assyrian hands. Israel's security rested on the destruction of the empire. If Israel's God extended mercy to the oppressors, future generations of Israelites would be doomed. And, in the final writing of history, Jonah was right. God showed mercy to the Assyrians, sparing them, and within a generation, the Assyrian armies invaded, decimated, and scattered the northern kingdom of Israel. Jonah disobeyed God out of his deeper loyalty to his own people.

Jonah was far more comfortable with a God of justice than with a God of mercy. And many of us today, particularly those of us in marginalized communities, feel the same way. Why should Christians in marginalized communities of color, now more or less disempowered, bother with a biblical call to reach out to those who benefit from their racial and ethnic disenfranchisement? Why should they seek reconciliation with their oppressors? A very pragmatic reason is that to do nothing ensures the continuation of oppressive structures. Yet to rebel violently against the status quo only encourages the dominant culture, with its monopoly on power in the form of armies and police forces, to crush indiscriminately and mercilessly any opposition. Brazilian educator Paulo Freire maintains that "this then is the great humanistic and historical task of the oppressed, to liberate themselves and their oppressors as well. The oppressors, who oppress, exploit, and rape by virtue of their power, cannot find in this power the strength to liberate either the oppressed or themselves" (1994, 26). The hope of radically subverting and bringing about change in the way our political and economic structures are constructed lies with the liberation of those complicit with the structure of oppression.

Attention should be given to the pronouncements of Jesus and particularly to one of his memorable conversations with Peter. "Then Peter came up to Jesus and said, 'Lord, how often shall my sibling sin against me and I forgive? Until seven times?' Jesus said to him, 'I do not say to you until seven times, but until seventy times seven'" (Matt. 18:21-22). But what happens if by forgiving the enemy we end up condemning our own people? How can we lay claim to the radical teaching of Jesus if, like Jonah, we attempt to maintain loyalty to our own oppressed group? These are difficult questions to answer.

Any understanding of the biblical mandate to forgive and to reconcile forces a deeper look at today's crucified people. Those crucified by racist, ethnic, or sexual discrimination in our time are also heirs of Jesus's ministry. The writer of the Epistle of

James instructs, "Did not God choose the poor of this world to be rich in faith and heirs of the reign which God promised to those loving God?" (2:5). Jesus said that the poor are those who should be happy for theirs is the kingdom of God, and those who are rich in power and privilege now have their consolation (Luke 6:20-21, 24-25). All those complicit with structures of oppression, poor and rich alike, have no claim to God's eschatological promise of salvation as reconciliation.

Merely believing in Jesus as savior is insufficient for obtaining salvation, liberation, or reconciliation. Does not the author of the letter of James warn us that even the demons believe in Jesus and tremble at his name? (2:14-20, 24, 26). Concentrating solely on a Christ divorced from praxis only encourages "cheap grace," whether among the disenfranchised or among those complicit with oppressive structures. Faithfulness to the gospel message requires moving beyond a belief in Jesus to a response to Jesus's activities aimed at justice and reconciliation. Jonah's belief in God was insufficient. His faithfulness to God's message could only be ascertained through the action of entering the city of Nineveh and proclaiming God's mercy. For the marginalized to continue simply worshiping Christ without justice-seeking actions contributes to maintaining the present sociopolitical structures of oppression. To follow Jesus, to be called one of his disciples, is to be called to struggle with Christ's crucified people for salvation, liberation, and reconciliation. To oppose reconciliation is to deny Christ's message, regardless of whether a belief in Christ is professed or Christ's name is proclaimed on one's lips as the source of salvation.

The marginalized cannot hate their oppressors and claim to love or belong to God, for as John reminds us, "Anyone who says, I love God and hates his or her sibling, is a liar; if they cannot love the sibling they see, how can they love God who cannot be seen? This commandment we have from [Jesus]: The ones loving God also love their siblings" (1 John 4:20-21). Those who claim to be Christians are called to love those complicit with oppressive structures because God is also in them. Borrowing from the Christian mystics' concept of panentheism, we recognize the paradoxical mystery of God's transcendence and immanence. Paul Tillich, who subscribed to panentheism, explained that God does not merely exist as finite beings exist. Instead, God is the base for everything existing. While present within everything, God is not to be equated with the all (1969, 82). The importance of panentheism is God's presence in the Other, as well as the non-Other. The mandate to love our enemies, regardless of whether they deserve our love or not, is based on the presence of God, the *imago Dei*, in them. This is why we are called to reconcile with all our brothers and sisters. But how can marginalized communities learn to love those oppressing them?

Theologian Mark Kline Taylor uses the term "christopraxis" to describe actions arising from the faith community's commitment to Jesus Christ. While praxis is central to any response to the gospel message, it is Christ-centered action that originates within a faith community that is totally devoted to the thinking of Jesus. Such actions take precedence over theory (1990, 18-19). Or, as Leonardo Boff reminds us, "Our task is not to do Christology, but to follow Christ" (1978, 231).

While an overall commitment to die to one's power and privilege remains for those who benefit from the present oppressive social structures, christopraxis for the marginalized requires a change of heart toward the beneficiaries of empire. Specifically, it requires learning how to love one's enemies, even when those enemies fail to acknowledge their wrongdoing, repent, and seek forgiveness. To love those whom we hold responsible for real and deep pain is more for our sake than for theirs, as we will explore in the next chapter. The text calls all, beginning with the heirs to God's reign, to fulfill Christ's task of establishing justice.

Supposedly, Jesus proclaimed a new commandment to be followed by all those who would be called by his name. Matthew records Jesus saying: "You heard that it was said, 'You shall love your neighbor and hate your enemies.' But I say to you, love your enemies, bless those cursing you, do good to those hating you, and pray on behalf of those abusing and persecuting you, so that you may be children of your Father in Heaven" (5:43-45). How, then, do we demonstrate love for the oppressor? It cannot be by simply submitting to the oppression. Instead, the disempowered are required to struggle to restore the humanity of the powerful by fostering a justice that liberates not only the oppressed but also the oppressor. This is what it means to be fully human.

Any quest for justice cannot spiritualize love; love must be grounded and love must involve action. Often the scars of injustice are too deep, and the sorrow too wide, simply to forgive and forget. Yet, to allow our entire outlook to remain controlled by hatred and anger toward the dominant culture will prevent any type of meaningful dialogue. Revenge, then, becomes the only alternative left to us, and paths to reconciliation close. J. Deotis Roberts reminds us that "where there is no forgiveness, there is no repentance. If it is true that one who does not repent is not forgiven, it is likewise true that one who cannot forgive others cannot repent, for he or she does not have the sensibility to do so" (1994, 60). How, then, can we be faithful to the biblical mandate to love and reconcile in the midst of present power structures that continue to foster injustice?

Love, like reconciliation or salvation, is a divine eschatological act of God. The author of the Second Letter to the Corinthians wrote, "So if anyone is in Christ, that one is a new creation; the old things have passed away, and behold, all things have become new! All things are of God, having reconciled us to Godself through Jesus Christ, and having given us to the ministry of reconciliation, for God was in Christ reconciling the world to Godself, not charging them their sins but putting in us the word of reconciliation" (5:18-19). The locus of God's new creation of reconciliation is in the ministry of God's people. However, before the momentous step of loving our enemies can ever be taken, we must reaffirm our loyalty and love for the marginalized within our disenfranchised communities. If our ultimate aim is reconciliation, void of revenge, then we must learn how to love our enemies as ourselves. But, before we can be trusted with this task, we must begin the short-term goal of loving and learning from those who reside within our own marginalized communities.

Our commitment to unmasking, debunking, and dismantling racism and ethnic discrimination becomes the necessary christopraxis—action in Christ—that will teach us how to expand a sense of justice to include those of the oppressive dominant cul-

ture. The task of loving our enemies, we must confess, seems
beyond our abilities. But *if* through Christ all things are possible,
then it becomes critical that we fully understand the model of
Jesus presented in the gospels.

THE JESUS MODEL

Those wishing to ground their understanding of reconciliation
within the Christian tradition are forced to deal with the figure of
Jesus Christ. All accounts concerning Jesus reveal a person who
both offered and demanded that all who would call themselves
his disciples offer unconditional forgiveness, regardless of whether
the offender asked for or even recognized the need for forgiveness. Jesus also proscribed vengeful retaliation for wrongs committed, for "vengeance is mine" says the Lord (Rom. 12:19). The
very heart of the gospel message, even for the enemy who refuses
the gift of grace, is reconciliation, specifically the turning away
from evil, seeking forgiveness of sins, and turning toward a new
life in and through Jesus Christ.

Text after text shows a Christ who offered forgiveness as a way
of bringing the offender to repentance. Reconciliation implies the
eschatological state of salvation. As Paul reminds us, "Yet while
we were still sinners Christ died for us. . . . For while being enemies, we were reconciled to God through the death of God's son,
much more being reconciled we shall be saved by his life" (Rom.
5:8, 10). Therefore, we are to "Forbear one another and forgive
each other. Just as Christ forgave you, so too you forgive" (Col
3:13). Jesus couldn't be any clearer in his proclaiming of the Great
Commission: he sends out his disciples so that "in [Christ's] name,
repentance for the forgiveness of sins will be preached to all
nations" (Luke 24:47). In fact, all the Synoptic Gospels link God's
forgiveness of us to how we forgive those who have wronged us.
Matthew warns us, "*If* you forgive others their trespasses, your
heavenly Father will forgive you" (6:14).[8] The gospel stories

---

[8] According to Mark, "When you stand in prayer, if you have anything
against anyone, forgive them, so that your Father in heaven may forgive your

assume that only those who have experienced God's mercy are able to show mercy toward others. If extending God's mercy to others is absent, the question arises if an inward conversion has actually taken place. There really is no way around it—those choosing to call themselves Christians are called to embrace their enemies as God, through Christ, has embraced them.

Nevertheless, while it may be true that on that "last" day "the wolf shall dwell with the lamb, and the leopard shall lie down with the goat" (Isa. 11:6), it seems that until then, neither the lamb nor the goat will get much sleep. Surely they will be busy doing everything in their power to maintain a safe distance between themselves, for experience must have taught them to be leery of predators with a history of devouring them. In fact, any attempt on their part to pursue a relationship before "that day" may prove deadly. How, then, is the gospel mandate of reconciliation, as demonstrated in the life and actions of Christ, to be implemented in the reality of a continuous oppressive situation? Yes, mercy is to be extended, but so too is salvation. As already discussed, salvation as liberation from *all* sins, personal as well as communal, requires that the structures that create sin (oppression) must be dismantled so that those who benefit from these structures can, in fear and trembling, find their own salvation and humanity. Extending mercy and establishing justice are not part of an "either/or" proposition; instead, the praxis is one of "both and." The motif that God is a lover of justice is as important in biblical texts as the message of extending mercy to the enemy. "You are a ruler," sings the psalmist, "who loves justice, insisting on honesty, justice, and virtue" (Ps. 99:4).

Extending mercy and establishing justice must be simultaneous parts of the same praxis. True reconciliation, as theologian Juan Luis Segundo reminds us, is possible only if a genuine conversation has occurred. Such a conversation is conscious of the causes of the conflict and has moved to rectify them. If not, reconciliation would prematurely take place, masking the existing causes of

---

transgressions" (11:25). Luke writes, "Be merciful as your Father also is merciful. Do not judge and you will not be judged. Do not condemn, and you will not be condemned. Forgive and you will be forgiven" (6:36-37).

the conflict and making any just solution impossible to achieve (Segundo 1993, 37). But how is such a reconciliation achieved?

Jonah, unfortunately, provides us with a poor example. Not only did he end up sitting on a hill desiring God's wrath to descend on the wicked city of Nineveh; more important, he never bothered to seek the liberation of the oppressors by demanding that they practice justice. In his preaching of God's message, he did not explain why God was angered, just that this was so. Nowhere in his message did he hold the Ninevites accountable to any principles of justice. We need not follow Jonah's example but instead we can learn from his experience. And so we now turn to how reconciliation might actually be brought about.

4

Praying through Jonah

C AN WE TRULY BLAME J ONAH for refusing to deliver God's message of mercy to his archenemies? After all, Jonah is being asked to reach out to an empire whose very identity was forged in a deliberate attempt to conquer his people. Imagine a Jew, at the dawn of World War II, going to the capital of Nazi Germany to attempt to reason with Hitler. If we bring the analogy closer to home, Jonah going to Nineveh is akin to an African American going to the deep South in the 1920s to reconcile with the Ku Klux Klan, or for a Sioux warrior to approach the U.S. cavalry on the eve of the Wounded Knee massacre in the hope of understanding each other. As noble as such acts may sound, the end result, more often than not, is conquest or death for the messenger of hope. These are not meetings of equals attempting to work out their differences. These are encounters between the powerful bent on maintaining the subjugation of the "Other" by whatever means possible.

It is dangerous to assume that examples of brutality toward the marginalized are part of a less enlightened past. Surely physical atrocities committed toward blacks by the Klan, toward Native Americans by the U.S. cavalry, or toward Latino/as in the southwest by the Texas Rangers have ceased to be common occurrences. But as we saw in the second chapter, today's disenfranchised are lynched and massacred by economic systems. While it may be true that an empire today is less dependent on the systematic physical decimation of a people, the ultimate goal of harvesting talents, resources, labor, and bodies for the common good of the dominant Eurocentric culture continues as violence is institutionalized by economic means. Today, death for the marginalized will seldom come instantaneously at the end of a rope, or while huddled unarmed on a field by a frozen creek (although such a fate may await undocumented workers in this country), but it comes prematurely nevertheless, through the poverty of the ghettos, reservations, and *barrios*.

What, then, does it mean to ask today's U.S. marginalized communities of color to forgive those who continue to benefit from their disenfranchisement and seek reconciliation? Like the Assyrians of old, today's dominant U.S. culture is not asking for forgiveness, nor does it see any need to repent—especially if such repentance would lead to a new social order that could jeopardize its power and privilege. Take the example of Southern Baptists, the largest Christian denomination in the United States, with an estimated 15.6 million members.[1] In 1845, the Southern Baptists split from their northern counterparts over the issue of slavery, specifically, over debate as to whether a slaveholder could be appointed as a missionary to Africa. After the Civil War, Southern Baptists had a hand in establishing the Ku Klux Klan. It should not be surprising that it was normative for Southern Baptists to oppose civil rights during the 1950s and 1960s by supporting segregation. As late as the 1970s, many churches excluded blacks from their congregations. Nevertheless, when the Southern Baptist Convention assembled in Atlanta in 1995, it issued the following apology to all African Americans for its racist past and asked for forgiveness.

> We lament and repudiate historic acts of evil such as slavery from which we continue to reap a bitter harvest, and we recognize that the racism which yet plagues our culture today is inextricably tied to the past; and . . . we apologize to all African-Americans for condoning and/or perpetuating individual and systemic racism in our lifetime; and we gen-

---

[1] For the record, it should be noted that I am an ordained Southern Baptist minister who has served as a church pastor.

uinely repent of racism of which we have been guilty, whether consciously or unconsciously.

The resolution received a standing ovation from the roughly twenty thousand delegates attending the convention. Accepting the apology, on behalf of all African Americans, was Gary L. Frost, the only black person at that time on the convention's executive committee.[2] But the question to consider is if Reverend Frost, or any other individual for that matter, can accept an apology for all the Africans who lost their lives during the Middle Passage? Can any one person speak for all the black women ever raped by their masters? Can one person truly represent the generations upon generations of slave descendants who have been systematically locked out of decent housing, education, and health care? In short, who can speak on behalf of the injured parties? To whom should the oppressor address such an apology, and who has the authority to forgive? In addition, when we consider that a vast majority of Southern Baptists are religious and political conservatives who usually vote for political candidates and policies that are detrimental to people of color, we must ask what good their apology accomplishes if they continue to support political initiatives that reinforce the racism and ethnic biases of the present social structures.

A more recent example occurred in the Church of England, which voted in February of 2006 to acknowledge its historical complicity in the global slave trade. "Complicity" seems a very mild term considering that the Church's Society for the Propagation of the Gospel in Foreign Parts owned and operated slave-holding sugar plantations in the Caribbean. Slaves at these plantations were branded with red-hot irons so that the word "Society" appeared on their chests. When slavery was finally abolished, plantation owners—but not the slaves—were compensated.[3] Apologies are always nice, but, as Archbishop Desmond Tutu reminds us, "If you take my pen, what good does

---

[2] "Southern Baptists Condemn Slavery," *Virginian-Pilot*, June 21, 1995.

[3] Thomas Wagner, "Anglicans to Apologize for Role in Slave Trade," *Denver Post*, February 9, 2006.

an apology do, if you still keep my pen?" (Kidwell et al. 2001, 170).

The question before U.S. marginalized communities of color that claim Christian identity is *how* to take seriously the biblical motif of reconciliation. What responsibilities and duties do victims of oppression have toward their tormentors? Even the most superficial readings of biblical texts, particularly in the New Testament, emphasize the praxis of bountiful mercy, undeserved forgiveness, unconditional love, and everlasting reconciliation. So, to return to the question, can we truly blame Jonah for refusing to deliver God's message of mercy to his archenemies? How many among the oppressed today would join Jonah in attempting to escape to Tarshish? How many would choose to flee the presence of God rather than witness the redemption of those complicit with so much death and misery? Is this radical mandate of the gospel too radical? How, then, can disenfranchised groups of color approach the biblical call for reconciliation? The first step is to determine exactly what we mean by the term "reconciliation."

DEFINING CHRISTIAN RECONCILIATION

Any attempt to define reconciliation must begin with the realization that no two situations are alike. Just as there is no single monolithic disenfranchised U.S. group, there is no monolithic understanding of reconciliation. Any process seeking reconciliation must remain contextual to that particular situation and those particular needs. The focus of this book is racial and ethnic reconciliation between the powerful and the powerless in the United States. In this country, power relationships are distributed differently than in other parts of the world, and thus the search for a more just society can be expected to differ as well. Although marginality is often the link that causes some U.S. groups to share the consequences of disenfranchisement with the peoples of other continents, the causes of oppression likely differ in their histories, and any movement from oppression to reconciliation must remain embedded in the particular social customs, traditions, and norms of that location. While common goals, hopes, and aspirations may be shared, in the end the methods of finding healing, establishing justice, and securing peace will and must differ.

It is also important to emphasize that bringing about reconciliation is not easy: the process can be complicated and at times even contradictory. This chapter's attempt to describe, formulate, and seek reconciliation offers, at best, loose guidelines to consider, debate, and adjust so as to meet the physical and spiritual health of particular communities. I am not presenting doctrines, road maps, or blueprints for Christians on how to achieve reconciliation; rather, I am struggling to provide possible approaches and models grounded in biblical ethics.

It may be helpful to begin by stating clearly what reconciliation is not. Reconciliation is not a once-and-for-all moment at which a conflicted society suddenly arrives: rather, it is a lifelong process that can transcend generations. Will those of us working in ethics today see a new social order based on justice toward people of color? Probably not. Then why should we struggle for reconciliation and continue to hope against all hope? We work toward reconciliation, peace, and justice because it is our Christian calling and so that our children and our children's children might partake of justice and peace from the seeds we plant today. The call for reconciliation is a project whose fruits will be harvested in the future. However, results we may witness today might include a relaxation of oppressive social norms and a reduction in death-inducing legislation on issues related to education, health care, and equal employment opportunities. Such actions, however, should never be confused with reconciliation. They are but preliminary steps toward that end.

Any definition of reconciliation must arise within marginalized communities. Those who presently benefit from the existing social order lack the objectivity and moral authority to define reconciliation or even recognize the need for reconciliation. We would be hard-pressed to find an example in history where those in power willingly relinquished their privileged positions for the sake of justice. It seems that power must always be wrested away, so that demands for justice can be heard. Reconciliation must always start with the victims of abusive power structures. This is why Jonah was sent by God to prophesy to Nineveh and to call the Assyrian empire to repentance for the oppression it had unleashed on the people of other nations. If those in power are left to define the reconciliation process, the end result could very well be a truce in which the prevailing social structures that brought about injustices are not examined, challenged, nor changed.

However we decide to define reconciliation, it is clear that reconciliation must originate from within the marginalized communities. Reconciliation is not simply what God does, but rather what marginalized communities do to remain faithful to God's call for liberation from all forms of sin—sins of the individual, and sins of the community imposed upon the life of the individuals. Unfortunately, the normative approach to reconciliation has been those with power—those who have created division and hatred within society—attempting to make peace with those from whom they have taken or withheld power.

One of the most effective strategies of those with power is to sustain strife and division that may already exist among communities of color. This is usually a struggle among the have-nots for the crumbs that fall from the master's table. Government and religious institutions usually relegate only a small portion of their resources to meet the needs and concerns of minorities, who are then forced to resort to competing and even fighting among themselves for the resources. When competition is fostered among marginalized communities, the disenfranchised are unlikely to work together. This in turn secures the dominance of Euroamericans within the country. Such a strategy is crucial as accelerating demographic shifts create a new America in which Euroamericans cease to be the majority.

Differences do exist among races and ethnicities, but this should not become a barrier. Continuous division among marginalized groups prevents the disenfranchised from accumulating the critical mass needed to challenge effectively those who benefit from the present power structures. Fostering animosities between marginalized groups by carefully disbursing economic privilege does no more in the end than secure and protect the power and privilege of the dominant culture. I agree with James Cone's assertion in 1975 that the first task in the process of reconciliation with the dominant power should be to find reconciliation among ourselves (1975, 245). At the time Cone was writing from a white/black dichotomy, addressing "among ourselves" to the black community; today, however, we must be inclusive of all communities of color.

However reconciliation is defined, it should never be confused with an absence of hostility. This is pacification and not reconciliation. Nor should it be understood as an attempt to pacify the victims of social structures *without* dealing with the structures responsible for much of the disenfranchisement. All too often reconciliation is reduced to negotiation, a bargaining process with the goal of reducing hostility, but with minimal change. Most often the goal of such an undertaking is not to bring forth justice and liberation, but to manage the disenfranchised so that they better accept the prevailing social order. The goal of reconciliation, however, whether in the time of the prophets or today, must be to establish justice and peace. There can be no reconciliation as long as power structures that continue to benefit the few at the expense of the many remain in place.

Further, we must recognize that reconciliation cannot be limited to the spiritual domain. Reconciliation is a physical process, a process of flesh and blood struggling for liberation from an oppressive status quo. All too often reconciliation is spiritualized. People from different races and ethnicities are envisioned holding hands and singing together a song such as "Kumbaya, my Lord, Kumbaya," a phenomenon witnessed during numerous Promise Keepers rallies that drew predominantly white men. While some people of color were prominently displayed to give the illusion of racial and ethnic reconciliation, the reality is that once the rally was over, the white men returned to their predominantly white neighborhoods and reported their successes in racial reconciliation to their predominantly white churches. Romanticized notions of racial and ethnic reconciliation always mask oppressive structures with political correctness or superficialities. Centering reconciliation on the far less appealing actual work, the physical struggle to overcome disempowerment and poverty that is the struggle for justice, is the only way reconciliation can become a reality or bring about lasting change.

HUMANIZING THE OPPRESSOR

Jonah shakes his fist at God, angry that God's divine mercy detracts from God's divine justice. The Assyrians, in Jonah's mind, are pure evil, undeserving of any compassion or mercy. Because they are monsters, not humans, they deserve retribution, justice that is quick and stiff. But what Jonah and others today who have suffered unjustly at the hands of oppressors fail to realize is that the sin of domination not only dehumanizes the life of the oppressed, but it also reduces the life of the oppressor. According to Rabbi Scherman, "The Hebrew word for sin, *hātā*ʾ literally means 'lack,' 'a diminution.' The act of sin *in itself* diminishes the sinner. It makes him [or her] a lesser human being. It engenders within him [or her] an indifference to evil, a tolerance for evil, an appetite for evil—and eventually, a distaste for good" (1978, xli). Sin becomes more than simply what an individual does: it is what an individual becomes.

If we can agree that unjust social structures are in themselves sinful, mainly because they prevent humans from achieving the full potential for which God created them, then we must seek repentance and turn away from this particular sin. We must look instead toward a new reality based on justice for all. Reconciliation is more than a simple offer of forgiveness. It is a process of changing the political, social, and economic power relationships that presently exist between those who benefit from the prevailing order and those who exist on its underside. It is the process of achieving a more human existence for the victims, previously treated as nonhumans, and their masters, who through their actions have made themselves inhuman. Some will be lifted up and some will be brought down so that all become more fully human. This process is described in the words of Mary, the mother of Jesus, in the Magnificat: "[God] brings down the powerful ones from thrones, and exalts the marginalized. God fills the hungry with good things, and sends away the rich empty-handed" (Luke 1:52-53).

It is easy (and yes, even justifiable at times) to feel anger, bitterness, and even hatred toward those who continue to benefit from the disenfranchisement of others. But dangers, both physical and emotional, exist if these feelings are left to fester, and hope for a lasting justice may wither, as did the bush that offered brief protection to Jonah. It is important to acknowledge that the acts of both demonizing oppressors and dehumanizing victims stunt any hope for communications that can lead to a reconciled future that encompasses a more just social order. This is not to say that prevailing structures of power are not demonic; certainly they can be, as is indicated by the misery and death (literally and figuratively) they foster. But those who benefit from these demonic structures are not themselves necessarily demonic. While some may be aware of the outcomes of their actions, the vast majority are undoubtedly simply ignorant. Their salvation lies in having their consciousness raised.

If hatred is not an appropriate response, what would be? The same responses that God probably sought from Jonah: compassion and pity. Pity for their lack of humanity and their inability to gain salvation. Pity for the masks of superiority they are forced to wear. Compassion that they too are trapped in a harmful construct of reality. Pity that by continuously profiting at the expense of their marginalized neighbors, they have become disconnected from their own spirituality. Pity for how they justify their undue power and privilege, for how they rationalize, and idealize the imbalance that benefits them—and lose God in the process.

The biblical model to consider is Jesus hanging on the cross, who took pity on his tormentors and cried out to heaven, "Father, forgive them, for they do not know what they are doing" (Luke 23:34). Unlike Jesus, Jonah failed to realize that the behavior of the people of Nineveh was enmeshed with the prevailing social structures of the Assyrian empire. From the cradle to the grave, their experiences within the empire reinforced the "rightness" of a lifestyle dependent on an underside of weaker neighbors. Jesus seemed to understand that people were shaped by the unjust norms of a dominant culture. He spoke out for the Samaritan, the woman about to be stoned for adultery, the ritually "unclean," even the tax collectors of the empire. He recognized sin in both people and systems. Jesus understood oppression, and he knew pain. So looking down from the cross at the Roman soldiers, Jesus expressed pity for them: they were following orders; they were acting without thinking; their actions were the natural consequences of their upbringing. This Jesus understood.

By consciously separating the actors from their actions, the oppressors from the evil of the oppressive structures, those privileged by empire can be seen for what they are: lost sinners separated from God and in need of God's love, grace, and salvation. They—whether the Assyrians of old or the neoliberals of today's transnational corporations—can be accompanied on the path to conversion. This cannot happen if we, like Jonah, express hatred and condemnation toward "them" as we focus only on our own liberation. The goal of justice can then become a more attainable hope only if we look beyond ourselves and our needs. Compassion and pity promote empathy instead of hatred. It is possible to condemn oppressive structures and still hold the agents of these structures accountable for their actions. This is the beginning of the path to reconciliation and of bringing grace, salvation, and liberation from evil to the oppressor and oppressed alike.

A person might ask why Christians living on the margins should be concerned with the welfare of their oppressors? Shouldn't they focus instead on their own marginalized communities? Jesus has demonstrated clearly that this is not an either/or choice. Christians can justify the domination of others as witnesses to a Constantinian Christianity. Nevertheless, oppressors must be led to understand that their actions diminish their own humanity as well as that of their victims. As Episcopal priest Michael Battle reminds us, because all are created in God's image, all can find salvation, liberation, and redemption (2000, 172-82).

FORGIVING AND FORGETTING?

The victims of an unjust history must be allowed to suffer, to grieve over what was lost and what can never be restored. To rush to "forgive and forget" trivializes their pain. This amounts to pacification without liberation. All too often those who benefit from unjust social structures are the first to call for reconciliation, but for a reconciliation that does not hold them culpable for what has taken place and a reconciliation that allows them simply to move on without giving up the very oppressive structures that continue to benefit them. But "good" Christians willing to "forgive and forget" so they can get on with their unexamined, unchallenged, and unchanged lives cannot bring about justice. Religious scholar Tink Tinker reminds us:

> We [Native Americans] stand as a source of judgment over against the continued Amer-European occupancy of North America. We will always present Americans with a choice. Either confess and acknowledge that history and move beyond it in a constructive, healing way, or engage the addicts' device of denial and keep those memories deeply suppressed and repressed where they will continue to fester and disrupt all of American life and well-being. (2004, 244)

To refuse to forget is to insist that the causes of injustice be fully examined and named, and then addressed through shifts in how power and privilege are distributed within the overall society, a process in which most beneficiaries of power do not wish to engage.

Refusing to Forgive

Oppressors require redemption. The perplexing problem oppressors face is how to obtain forgiveness without having to sacrifice accumulated wealth and privilege. If only the disenfranchised could be persuaded that it is their Christian duty to forgive. All that would be required, then, from oppressors would be the tearful offering of an apology, which could be accepted by a token member of a marginalized group and consummated with a "brotherly" hug. Once forgiven for past mistakes, the oppressors could get on with their lives without the inconvenience of having to deal with restitution or to worry about how to restructure the divisions of power to forge a more just social order. However, such easy forgiveness can lead only to what Adam Clayton Powell Sr. termed "cheap grace" for the oppressor, and it would continue the oppression of the marginalized. Cheap grace simply masks the underlying causes of the pain, suffering, and misery the disenfranchised are forced to endure. Premature offering of forgiveness serves neither the cause of reconciliation nor justice.

Reverend Adam Clayton Powell Sr., the renowned and dynamic pastor of Abyssinian Baptist Church of Harlem, coined the term "cheap grace" to refer to white Christian America's tolerance of Jim Crow, lynching, and racism. Dietrich Bonhoeffer, who is usually associated with the term "cheap grace," learned this ethical principle from Powell while attending his church during his student days at Union Theological Seminary. Probably for the first time in Bonhoeffer's life, he witnessed the social gospel in action, experiencing a faith community engaged in dismantling the racist political and social structures of its time. Bonhoeffer was able to transport the lessons learned from the black church to deal with the rising anti-Semitism of his native Germany (Clingan 2002, 4).[4] Witnessing the seduction of many of his compatriots by Hitler's National Socialism, Bonhoeffer boldly denounced Hitler as a false god intent on creating a history devoid of God. The 1937 publication of Bonhoeffer's *Nachfolge* laid out the cost of Christian discipleship. Although his opposition to Nazism would eventually earn him martyrdom, the lessons learned from the black church continue to live today. For him, the grace of God and the forgiveness of sins were free, but never cheap. He wrote:

> Cheap grace is the deadly enemy of our Church. We are fighting today for costly grace. . . . The essence of grace, we suppose, is that the account has been paid in advance; and, because it has been paid, everything can be had for nothing. . . . Cheap grace means the justification of sin without the

---

[4] Most scholarship on Bonhoeffer's six months at Abyssinian Baptist Church in New York City concentrates on how the church's worship style influenced his ethical thinking. Passionate Black music and emotional manifestations during services appear as the focus of most discussions of Bonhoeffer's time at Abyssinian. It is interesting to note that few Euroamerican scholars are willing to explore the intellectual contributions the black church, and Adam Clayton Powell in particular, made to Bonhoeffer's scholarly development. We are left asking why?

justification of the sinner. Grace alone does everything, they say, and so everything can remain as it was before. . . . Cheap grace is the preaching of forgiveness without requiring repentance. . . . Cheap grace is grace without discipleship, grace without the cross, grace without Jesus Christ, living and incarnate. . . . [But] costly grace is the gospel which must be *sought* again and again. . . . Such grace is *costly* because it calls us to follow, and it is *grace* because it calls us to follow *Jesus Christ*. . . . It is costly because it condemns sin, and grace because it justifies the sinner. Above all, it is *costly* because it cost God the life of [God's] son . . . and what has cost God much cannot be cheap for us. (1963, 45-48)

Simple forgiveness short-circuits the hope of establishing the reign of God. It encourages what Powell, and later Bonhoeffer, calls "cheap grace," costing the perpetrator nothing and maintaining the very societal structures responsible for oppression in the first place. At the end of the last century and the beginning of this one, it has become "politically correct" for a dominant group to publicly confess its past transgressions, receive public affirmation for humbling itself, and thus, with forgiveness in hand, move on. This often obviates any need to consider or analyze the reasons for the oppression—indeed, this may be the intention from the beginning. The focus then shifts from the one who has been transgressed against to the one who benefits from the transgression. Such a focus is not only insulting to the one who has been abused, but it is likely to inflict greater pain as this "cheap grace" replaces any hope of creating a truly just social order.

Nonetheless, the biblical text does call for forgiving those who trespass against us. And Jesus reminds us, "Be on your guard; if your brother or sister sins against you, rebuke them, and if they repent, forgive them. And if seven times a day they sin against you, and seven times a day turn to you saying 'I repent,' you shall forgive them" (Luke 17:3-4). Jesus sets a pattern by which forgiveness is to be offered. It is not simply offered when the oppressor apologizes, but is rather a step in a process: the offender is first rebuked, the offender must then repent, and finally forgiveness is offered. This three-step process is the basic pattern to be followed in all quests for reconciliation. Countries that have undergone periods of brutal oppression have incorporated this model in the form of Truth and Reconciliation commissions to deal with the past. Commission hearings in Argentina, Chile, El Salvador, Fiji, Ghana, Guatemala, Liberia, Morocco, Panama, Peru, Sierra Leone, South Africa, South Korea, and East Timor have all provided public forums where the oppressed can tell their stories, rebuke those responsible for their sufferings, and hopefully provide an opportunity for repentance and forgiveness. Unfortunately, the United States has yet to see a need for establishing its own national Truth and Reconciliation commission to deal with its own past (and present) racism and ethnic discrimination.

Jesus calls us to forgive those who have offended us, but who can offer forgiveness to those who have sinned against an entire community? The Gospel of Luke recounts that one day Jesus was teaching God's word at the home of friends when a few men appeared, carrying a paralyzed man upon a cot, whom they hoped to bring to Jesus for healing. When the large crowd made it impossible to reach Jesus, they climbed up onto the flat roof, removed some tiles, and lowered the paralyzed man on his stretcher into the midst of the gathering. Seeing their faith, Jesus responded, "My friend, your sins are forgiven." Among the crowd were some Pharisees and doctors of the law, who thought to themselves, "Who does this man think he is, speaking blasphemy? No one can forgive sins except God alone." But Jesus replied that the "Son" had been given authority to forgive sins (Luke 5:17-24a). And the people left, glorifying God.

Both the Hebrew Bible and the New Testament agree that it is God and God alone who can ultimately forgive sins. No matter how personal an offense may be, there are always communal consequences to sin. All sins, but specifically sins of oppression and injustice, can impact an entire society, not just for this generation but for many generations to come. If a slaveholder, for example, were to repent, set his or her slaves free, and ask for their forgiveness, would they have the power or right to offer forgiveness and thus redemption? Even if they were to offer forgiveness for their own mistreatment, would they be able to speak for the slaves who came before them and suffered or died under this master's whip? As we have already pointed out, the suffering of victims of oppression, such as slaves, is often passed on to their descendants. They are likely to be disenfranchised by unequal access to health care, housing, and education simply because they are the children of slaves and unable to participate freely in the opportunities society has to offer. Nor could these "freed" slaves speak for others who have been directly disenfranchised by the action of this particular slaveholder or of other slaveholders.

Sociopolitical sins that foster societal injustices cannot be reduced to an individual matter between one oppressor and a certain number of those marginalized by the oppressor's actions. Biblical texts make this clear. The only one who can offer complete forgiveness and redemption is God. We humans are too limited; we are too human.

Alexander Pope probably said it best: "To err is human, to forgive divine." God's ability to offer unconditional forgiveness may never be possible for humans, but that is acceptable. Oppressive abuse may be so damaging that healing for the victim may never occur in his or her lifetime. While offering individual forgiveness may lead the victim toward healing, the healing process will never be completed if forgiveness is demanded or coerced: for example, "If you really are a Christian you would forgive and get over it." Still, the hope of healing and reconciliation is that one day the victim may come to the point where the offering of individual forgiveness is possible. Such forgiveness must not be for the sake of the powerful or privileged, but for the sake of the one who has been injured. Reconciliation is first and foremost about the healing of the victims, not absolution for those whose consciences are troubled or burdened with guilt.

At least two cautions should be noted. First, it would be wrong to place the burden of offering forgiveness on the shoulders of those who may not yet have experienced healing. And although it is true that healing can be accelerated if the victim of abuse offers forgiveness, in the messiness of life, the one abused may simply not be ready to offer forgiveness. More time may be required. Second, forgiveness can also be withheld in circumstances that would place the person abused in a more vulnerable situation, such as a battered wife forgiving a husband who sees no reason to repent.

The ability to offer forgiveness must remain a divine gift, with the offering of individual forgiveness mainly for the healing of the one who was and continues to be disenfranchised. As with the example of a single slaveholder requesting forgiveness from her or his slaves, it should be noted that if and when God forgives, redemption can be manifested only through the overall faith community, not the individual. The community is needed for accountability.

Refusing to Forget

Racial and ethnic strife still plague our land because the dominant culture of primarily Euroamericans refuses to remember what the marginalized can never forget, thus making reconciliation an elusive project. Not only can the marginalized not forget; they cannot simply bury the past. To do so would trivialize the trials and tribulations experienced by their ancestors and the continuing consequences faced by people of color today. Forgetting erases memory, betrays the past, and dishonors identity. Yet memory, as pastoral theologian Sharon Thornton reminds us, "can reveal the lie of injustice and open up a way to imagine a different future. . . . A vision of a new reality where people are released from the powers and principalities that crush and wound is a powerful force of resistance against injustices that cause and perpetuate suffering" (2002, 134).

Theologian Nigel Bigger provides three reasons why deliberate forgetting can never be an option.

First, some may be able to forget; but not, I think, the victim. Second, if government does not attend to the victims and their injuries, then it fails in one of its most basic political duties; for protecting and upholding victims of injury is one of the basic *raisons d'être* of the state. And third, grievances without redress tend to fester. Festering, they help to infect future generations with an indiscriminate hatred of the perpetrators and their descendants—and also with an endemic mistrust of the state that, having failed in its duty to vindicate victims past, seems ready to tolerate the injury of victims future. (2003, 5)

Forgetting is often what the dominant culture wants and attempts to impose through offers of forgiveness. Forgetting prevents the first action for justice from taking place: there must be public recognition of the victims' oppression and an accompanying acknowledgment of their dignity and self-worth. To forget is to dismiss the suffering and pain of marginalized communities. To forget is to question their passion for justice and to reduce their call for a more just society to ill-informed, inadequate, or overly sensitive opinions.

In the meantime, what the dominant culture chooses to remember is itself a re-membered or a dis-membered illusion, a fantasy created in the imagination of Euroamericans. The "American dream" where anyone willing to work hard can make it, in one form or another, has lasted centuries. This imaginary space is superimposed on those who live on the underside of that dream. Those on the underside then become further marginalized by being regarded as objects, with the possibilities of the dominant culture projected upon them: "We did it; why can't they?" Yet these fantasies have nothing to do with the reality of the lives of people marginalized by social structures.

THE IMPORTANCE OF HISTORY

If we define history as the memory of a people, albeit at times a history made toxic by false memories, how do the marginalized recall a history apart from what is imposed upon them by the dominant culture? Can a history exist that has not succumbed to the pressure to forget a past characterized by conquest, enslavement, and disenfranchisement? How can the marginalized retrieve a memory that will serve as the impetus to struggle for a reconciled justice? The goal should be faithful to the biblical paradigm presented in Galatians, where, since Christians are one body in Christ, distinctions are eliminated between "male and female" (sexism), "Jew and Greek" (racism), and "slave and master" (classism) (Gal. 3:28).

Retelling stories can be a primary step in resisting the false histories that are imposed upon marginalized communities. Edward Said was correct in insisting that "the idea that resistance, far from being merely a reaction to imperialism, is an alternative way of conceiving human history" (1993, 216). Recalling the truth of ignored and forgotten history provides a basis for resistance and also demonstrates that structures causing marginalization are not recent phenomena, but rather deep-seated practices traceable to the very foundation of Euroamerica. In short, recalling the truth, even of unrecognized memories, as Jesus reminds us, "shall set you free" (John 8:32).

Those whose history is one of suffering so others can benefit are called to be martyrs, not victims, to the truth. To be a martyr (Greek *martys;* pl. *martyres*), is to be a witness. Jesus's last words to his disciples prior to his ascension were "you will be my *martyres* (my witnesses) . . . to the ends of the earth" (Acts 1:8). To remember is to refuse victimhood and, instead, to choose to be a witness to the truth so that the perpetrators of the sin of oppression can come to repentance and salvation. But more important than the hope that members of the dominant culture will regain the God they have exchanged for power and privilege is that those who refuse to forget their history can find healing from past traumas through the act of remembering. Trying to forget past traumas is pointless and will likely lead to emotional consequences for the individual and society at some future time. Clinical psychologist Brandon Hamber insists that "the past will not let itself be ignored." Hamber maintains that psychological restoration and healing occur only when survivors of abuse are provided with a space to remember their suffering. To be heard, in detail, contributes to a collective healing process that publicly condemns the past while attempting to prevent future violations (2003, 158-59). To be a martyr, a witness to history, fulfills Jesus's last command to his followers and begins the process of healing for those abused by history. It also provides hope for the oppressor and points the way to reconciliation.

An accurate history of marginality also challenges the constructed history of the dominant culture. According to Frantz Fanon, this is a history where the dominant culture does not write a history "of the [ones] which he plunders but the history of his own [people] in regard to all that she skims off, all that she violates and starves" (1963, 51). The history of those oppressed by Euroamericans is clouded over or even buried in the history created by the United States. U.S. history is, in short, the history of a dominant power. Before this power's subjective "We the people," all nonwhites occupy the space "We are not." For any theological or biblical reflection about reconciliation to be relevant to the marginalized, the identity of this "We are not" constructed by the dominant "We," must be debunked. This can only occur by not forgetting! Exposing the social fabrication of the "We" disrupts the prevailing normalization of racial and ethnic distinctions and unveils the hidden dynamics of oppression.

Establishing an empire or a dominant culture is usually based on what Homi Bhabha, the colonial and postcolonial theorist, terms the "syntax of forgetting" (1994, 160-61). Nation building is enabled by epic tales of triumphant wars, heroic figures, and awe-inspiring achievements that elevate the dominant culture while disenfranchising the history of the Other. In this country, the true histories of Native Americans, African Americans, Asian Americans, and Latino/as—in short, all potential obstacles to the dominant culture's goal of achieving ultimate power and privilege—were sacrificed to the history of the powerful. The national narrative of the United States not only disguises the complex political forces responsible for producing that history, but, even more important, it suppresses the racial divisions that were created from the beginning.

Influential French philosopher Michel Foucault maintains that the domination of certain people by others creates values, and historical writings then justify the values and social positions of their authors. Domination is not a "relationship" per se, but becomes fixed throughout history by means of meticulous procedures conferring and imposing rights on one group and obligations on another. The dominant culture reproduces itself in history and normalizes its power by engraving its memories on both things and bodies. In effect, "The body manifests the stigmata of past experience" (1984, 83-85). These "stigmatas," forced on the bodies of people of color, require debunking through their refusal to forget. The marginalized must identify the pain, the injustice, and the hurt for which they seek restoration and healing, and which have been obscured by the imposed narrative of the dominant culture.

The quest for redressing the historical causes of oppression disrupts the self-identity created by the dominant culture's narrative. The victors of American history have inscribed their genealogies upon the national epic, genealogies that emphasize military victories and political achievements. That this history has been constructed does not preclude its becoming "the" official history as it mirrors the actions and values of the forward-thrusting Euro-americans. All other histories are silenced, covered up, or denied in the hope that they will be forgotten.

However, as philosopher George Santayana aptly wrote, "Those who cannot remember the past are condemned to repeat it" (1936, 284). Forced forgetting also creates a collective bitterness and resentment among the abused that can flare up at any time in violent ways. In addition, because the history created by the dominant culture excludes marginalized recollections, it becomes a history devoid of a real subject, for the complete truth of the Euroamerican subject is missing. This is why it becomes crucial for the dominant group to enforce forgetfulness. Fanon explained this point quite eloquently:

Perhaps we have not sufficiently demonstrated that colonialism is not simply content to impose its rule upon the present and the future of a dominated country. Colonialism is not satisfied merely with holding a people in its grip and emptying the native's brain of all form and content. By a kind of perverted logic, it turns to the past of the oppressed people, and distorts, disfigures, and destroys it. This work of devaluing pre-colonial history takes on a dialectical significance today. (1963, 210)

The community-specific histories of marginalized groups must be recalled and addressed. Only the voices of those who have been removed from history and no longer inhabit it can critique those with power and privilege who have substituted their epic tales and memory for what actually happened. Recalling this forgotten history forces the dominant culture to view the marginalized as subjects like themselves, rather than events in the epic tales. Moreover, ignoring the voices of history's neglected can serve to justify yesterday's racial and ethnic domination and normalize today's continuation of that oppression, while preventing tomorrow's hope for liberation.

In 1985, Andean Indians wrote a letter to Pope John Paul II, signed by leaders of several Indian organizations. In part, the letter read:

> We, the Indians of the Andes and America, have decided to give you back your Bible, since for the past five hundred centuries it has brought us neither love, peace or justice. We beg you take your Bible and give it back to our oppressors, whose hearts and minds are in greater need of its moral teachings. As part of the colonial exchange we received the Bible, which is an ideological weapon of attack. The Spanish sword used in the daytime to attack and kill the Indians, turned at night into a cross which attacked the Indian soul. (Sugirtharajah 2001, 222)

Those who benefit from the present power structures do not know the history of those whose oppression made their privilege possible. Acknowledging the wrongdoings of the past creates the possibility for replacing privilege with love, peace, and justice.

But hasn't political correctness made us all aware that the genocide of indigenous populations was evil? Or that the enslavement of African Americans was not a bright spot in our national story? While we may already "know" this history, as John Paul

Lederach reminds us, "it is a very different social phenomenon to acknowledge [it]." To acknowledge the forgotten history of the disenfranchised requires a hearing and rehearing of their stories, a process that validates their experiences and feelings—a primary step toward healing broken relationships (1997, 26). Coming to terms with the history of the marginalized requires acknowledging that the present social structures are the end product of a history that the dominant culture would prefer to forget. While these events may have taken place in the past, the power and privilege wrung out of them continue to accrue and the descendants of those who suffered continue to suffer today. The beneficiaries of power and privilege thus have a moral responsibility to search for an accurate history. Acknowledgment of what actually happened provides those who continue to benefit from the present social structure with the opportunity to realize that through repentance they too can achieve salvation.

Acknowledgment of a wrong must precede knowledge of a need for repentance. The dominant culture is rebuked not so that the marginalized can feel better about themselves, but so that the issues that prevent justice from occurring can surface and be addressed; otherwise there will be no possibility of salvation for the marginalized or dominant culture. Reconciliation begins with truth-telling by the victims whose struggle for justice requires interaction with those privileged by society. Although the quest for justice also benefits the dominant culture, the focus of the reconciliation process must remain with the marginalized. Reconciliation must first bring healing to the victims, then to the rest of society, including those who benefit from the way the society is structured.

The collective memory of groups that have experienced oppression cannot be changed; it is a memory constructed of painful events. But how the past is remembered and dealt with can influence the future in a positive way. As the past is remembered, the dichotomies of "remember and revenge" and "forgive and forget" are not helpful and should be put aside. Biblical texts call Christians to an ongoing process of remembering, forgiving, and reconciling.

DECIDING TO FORGIVE

Once the atrocities of the past and present are remembered, a distinction must be made between individual forgiveness and the forgiveness that comes from the larger society. Recall that Jonah was not called by God to forgive the Assyrians; he was called to proclaim God's message to repent. Because Jonah did not want to see God's grace extend to the oppressors, he preached God's mercy reluctantly, hoping that his enemies would turn a deaf ear to God's message and destruction would follow. Jonah was undoubtedly aware that forgiveness was an option, that God could choose not to enforce justifiable retribution, but instead respond with mercy. This was contrary to Jonah's desires, for he craved righteous retribution. He wanted the Assyrians to pay, and pay dearly. For Jonah, as for many of us today, providing an opportunity for oppressors to obtain forgiveness (from us and God) can appear to sacrifice the experiences of our people and betray the memories of our ancestors. Even though forgiving one's enemies appears to be so contrary to Jonah's well-being, as well as to ours, this *is* the foundational message of Jonah's story and of the gospels.

The need to offer forgiveness presents a certain paradox. As noted earlier, an individual rarely can offer forgiveness on behalf of a group. Who could accept repentance for massacred ancestors? But if only the victim has the authority to forgive, how then can we move toward a reconciliation and justice? Here we must turn to scripture for help. For Christians, forgiving is a response to Jesus's dictate of "Love your enemies, bless those cursing you, do good to those hating you, and pray on behalf of those abusing and persecuting you" (Matt. 5:44). For this reason, three clarifications can be helpful. First, we must ensure that justice does not become the first casualty in the process of pursuing forgiveness and reconciliation. We must carefully distinguish between (1) offering individual forgiveness as a response to loving one's enemies, and (2) offering communal forgiveness as a response to the need for justice. These are two different things that occur at different times during the reconciliation process. For our purposes, we will begin with the individual. Second, we must distinguish between forgiveness being offered without repentance from the aggressor, and forgiveness that is withheld until justice is established. Again, understanding forgiveness in two separate ways, forgiveness without repentance can occur on the individual level as a step toward forgiveness on the communal level. Third, an offer of individual forgiveness does not necessarily mean that reconciliation has taken place. The two terms are not synonymous, for the former leads to the latter.

Individual Forgiveness

As an individual, what does it mean to forgive one's enemies as a response of love? For Jesus, love is *the* norm for Christian behavior, a power responsible for both the resurrection and creation, a movement that draws humanity toward unity with God. Love, as understood by Jesus, is not reduced to an emotional feeling or an abstract concept. Love is a verb; it is an action done by one to another. The love Jesus calls for is unconditional, a love given even when undeserved, a decision not to repay evil with evil. Christians are called to share this love because, as John's first epistle reminds us, "We love [God] because [God] first loved us" (1 John 4:19). Each individual has received God's love, and is called to share it with everyone, even one's tormentors! Refusing to forgive demonstrates a belief that the *imago Dei*, the very image of God, does not reside in all humans. Refusing to forgive confesses a belief that there exist those who are beyond God's love, mercy, and grace. Refusing to forgive is to walk with Jonah.

Although it may not be wise to impel an entire community, which may or may not include Christians, to love their persecutors as a response to the Christian message, it is proper for Christian members of a marginalized community to hold fellow Christians within that same community accountable to gospel ideals. As previously noted, those who benefit from oppressive structures lack all moral authority to hold anyone within marginalized communities accountable. The gospel prohibits them from judging others until they have first judged themselves (Matt. 7:3-5). It is those individuals on the margins who profess Christianity that are called to forgive.

Once we decide to forgive, the next question is who should be forgiven? Just as no one person can offer forgiveness for an entire group, no single member of the dominant Euroamerican culture can truly be held responsible for actions committed by the dominant culture. Throughout many years of teaching I have heard many white students claim that they cannot be held responsible for whites who held slaves more than a hundred and fifty years ago. A common response is "I never held slaves, so why must I pay for what others did?" Some claim to be blameless because their forefathers fought with the Union Army. Others state that their ancestors arrived in this country in the early twentieth century, long after the Civil War had ended. In a way, they are correct. They should no more be held accountable for the actions of others than you or I should be held accountable for the actions of our parents. But to simply dismiss culpability because an ancestral link cannot be found to a slaveholder (or Indian slayer for that matter) misses the point. The person is not individually being held accountable for the actions of his or her group or parents, the individual is being held accountable for complicity with the present-day social structures that continue to deprive that racial or ethnic group of privileges and benefits. The call to repentance is not for an act that occurred a century and a half ago, but for being complicit bystanders in oppressive acts occurring today and which are at times the consequences of past sins.

Forgiving those who benefit from the present social structures is a strategy that trades the present unjust structures for a chance to communicate in order to establish a justice that can lead toward reconciliation. Forgiving the enemy does not mean becoming friends with the oppressor. Rather, it means trading hatred and pain that can consume and damage the victim of oppression for something better. Forgiveness is an expression of loving one's enemies, a praxis committed for the well-being of the one needing forgiveness and, more important, for the one offering forgiveness. The Christian forgives as an act of self-empowerment, self-healing, and self-preservation. Forgiving is first and foremost the action of a victim attempting to move beyond the pain and suffering that come with oppressive structures in the hope of becoming an agent of reconciliation. Any benefits to the designers or perpetrators of present sinful structures are secondary, even though the hope of their salvation may very well rest on reconciliation with those on their underside.

Individual forgiveness is important because revenge enslaves. Revenge as a response to oppressive structures is both spiritually and pragmatically the wrong action to take. As Martin Luther King reminds us: "Returning hate for hate multiplies hate, adding deeper darkness to a night already devoid of stars. Darkness cannot drive out darkness; only light can do that. Hate cannot drive out hate; only love can do that. Hate multiplies hate, violence multiples violence, and toughness multiplies toughness in a descending spiral of destruction" (1963, 37). To participate in revenge or violence provides an excuse for those who have at their disposal the means and power to unleash even greater oppression against the disenfranchised. Revenge and violence only provoke greater diligence on the part of those fighting tooth and nail to preserve their undue privilege by whatever means possible.

Offering individual forgiveness is never an act of submission, but rather a process of pitting the totality of oneself against the social structures designed to privilege one group over another. The forgiveness of the oppressed is a subversive individual forgiveness that restores the individual's humanity while challenging the overall social system. Offering forgiveness has the potential to liberate and heal the abused victim. Healing becomes no longer contingent upon the wrongdoer's decision to repent, for waiting may take several lifetimes. And waiting while doing nothing can be perceived as an offer of blanket amnesty. Regardless of what actions the oppressor takes (or fails to take), the victim need not wait before seeking liberation from the consequences of oppression, particularly if an offer of forgiveness can prevent a life of resentment and bitterness. According to a study that synthesized more than twenty years of research conducted by Robert Enright and Richard Fitzgibbons (psychologist and a psychiatrist), the offer of forgiveness plays a pivotal role in helping those wronged achieve piece of mind, and positively deal with their anger so as to relieve depression and anxiety caused by wrongdoings (2000).

While direct causality between clinical disorders and holding on to negative emotions produced by systemic abuse may seem difficult to correlate, sufficient documentation exists to make such a link. Bitterness takes a toll on the body but also negatively impacts relationships. Even in situations where reconciliation may appear impossible—as today where the dominant culture remains largely unaware that sinful structures are responsible for much of today's disenfranchisement—offering forgiveness can provide the marginalized with inner transformation. Holding on to bitterness and resentment can also work against the goal of achieving a reconciled justice. For example, Emmett Till, the fourteen-year-old son of Mamie Till Mobley was brutally murdered in 1955. During her son's funeral service at the Pilgrim Baptist Church in Chicago, she stepped up to the pulpit and said, "I don't have a minute to hate. I'll pursue justice for the rest of my life" (West 2004, 20-21). And she did, until her death in 2003. The primary purpose of individual forgiveness must always be to restore personal dignity, release resentment, and liberate.

As already noted, no one has a right to forgiveness. Forgiveness cannot be demanded by those with power, nor can it be forced upon the powerless; to do so would only reinforce the trauma of the victim. Paul Coleman, a therapist who works with families, warns that in unequal power relationships, the one who holds power must accept more responsibility in the reconciliation process. Coleman insists that "a premature discussion of forgiveness insidiously places the entire burden for the resolution of the conflict on the person who sees himself or herself as the primary victim" (1998, 83). For Coleman, forgiveness is not a feeling, it is a choice that can become empowering.

In some cases victims are unable to offer forgiveness. Because reconciliation is a work of God, the victim must wait until God provides the necessary grace to be able to make the decision to offer forgiveness. Until then, offers of individual forgiveness must be withheld. Jesus has set a precedent for withholding forgiveness at certain times: "Those whose sin you forgive are forgiven, and those whose sin you retain, are retained" (John 20:23). The injured party must be allowed to move though the stages of bereavement for both what has been taken and what the future consequences will be. These stages include denial, anger, depression, and, it is hoped, acceptance—not acceptance of the present situation of oppression, but rather acceptance that the present situation is a reality that causes pain and disenfranchisement. Only when acceptance is reached can the offer of individual forgiveness become a possibility. Unfortunately, for some this may not occur in their lifetime. In addition, providing immediate forgiveness can rob offenders of the opportunity to consider seriously their complicity in the structures responsible for much of the institutionalized violence experienced on the margins of society. Forgiveness offered too soon aborts any opportunity for atonement and repentance on the part of the offenders.

Perhaps the most that can be done by those unable to offer individual forgiveness is to turn the matter over to God asking God to do the forgiving. The Letter of Jude notes that when the archangel Michael became engaged in an argument with the devil over the body of Moses, the angel dared not denounce or abuse the devil, nor was he able to reconcile with the powers of darkness. All he was able to say is, "Let the Lord correct you" (Jude 9-10). At times, this may be all that the disenfranchised can say, leaving their abusers in the hands of their God, recognizing that all forgiveness comes from God and asking God to actively participate in the reconciliation process. Even as Jesus hung on the cross, he did not directly forgive his tormentors but called upon God to do so. In the end, even though the offering of personal forgiveness remains impossible, leaving forgiveness up to God is a positive step toward some sort of reconciliation. This may well be the first step toward the day when the marginalized victim discovers the grace to offer forgiveness.

If They Repent

How much easier it is to offer individual forgiveness if there is assurance that those who benefit from injustices will repent. However, if repentance does not include a change of lifestyle, it is just the mouthing of meaningless words. Whenever one of my children is caught tormenting his or her sibling, I usually demand that an apology be offered. And while the offending child may voice an apology, it is obvious at times that the apology is meaningless. "I'm sorry," really means "I'm sorry I got caught," "I'm sorry you're so emotional about something I'm glad I did," or even, "I'm sorry you insist on holding me accountable—can we move on now?" Children, like many guilty adults simply want to move on without making any radical change.

The prophets of old criticized the Jews for reducing repentance before God for their transgressions to cultic rituals devoid of remorse. The prophet Isaiah demanded that the Israelites move beyond offering empty apologies by connecting repentance with social justice. Early on, Isaiah has God rejecting the "endless sacrifices" offered by the people, for God has grown tired and sick of the "blood of bulls and goats." What God wants is for assistance and justice to flow out to help the most marginalized segments of society. The people are called on "to do good, seek justice, help the oppressed, be just to the orphan, and plead for the widow." Then and only then, "though their sins be like scarlet, they shall become white as snow, though red as crimson, they shall be like wool" (Isa. 1:10-18).

Later Isaiah recounts that God dismisses the empty penitential fasting of the people:

> Is this the fast I choose, a penitential day for humans? To bow your head down like a reed, lying down in sackcloth and ashes? Is this fasting, an acceptable day to Yahweh? Is this not the fast I have chosen? To break unjust fetters and undo the thongs of the yoke, and to let the oppressed go free, and break every yoke. Is it not to break your bread with the hungry, and bring to your home the wandering poor? When will you clothe the naked you see, or hide yourself from your own kin? (Isa. 58:5-7)

The doing of social justice becomes the external manifestation of internal repentance. The prophet Micah wondered what to bring God as an offering for sin. Holocausts of one-year-old calves? Rams by the thousand? His firstborn? None of these was what God required, for God asks us "to do justice, to love mercy, and to walk humbly before your God" (Mic. 6:6-8).

Repentance is not an emotion, an apology, or an abstract state of mind. Repentance is a praxis, an action, something to be done to reestablish a moral order in personal relationships and responsibilities rather than simply presume mercy and grace. The Hebrew word used for repentance in scripture, *těshûbâ*, is derived from *shûb*, which connotes the concept of retracing one's steps back to the correct path. The Greek word used, *metanoia*, connotes the radical and costly attitude, direction, or path taken after arriving at a new way of thinking. Repentance is not only a turning away from sin; it is also a turning toward a new way of living in Christ. Too often, the quest for forgiveness is motivated by the needs and desire of the oppressors to be forgiven so as to ease their burdens of guilt. At the very least, repentance requires not only recognition that a person has caused the oppression of others, even if through complicity rather than direct action, but also a sense of remorse—remorse not only for the wrongdoing but also for the undue power and privilege he or she possesses. Repentance does not consist of one easy step: it requires a meaningful apology, followed by action either to repair the damage done and/or to dismantle the very structures that created privilege.

The focus here is not on the need for the victims of oppression to forgive, but rather on the oppressors' need to take the steps of repentance. Reconciliation can become a reality only when those who benefit from the present sociopolitical structures take stock of how these structures are designed to enhance their wealth, power, and privilege.

If They Don't Repent

What happens when those complicit with structures of oppression see no reason to repent? They may be ignorant of the way in which they are unjustly privileged, or they may simply prefer the current level of injustice because it rewards them with privilege or power. For members of the dominant Euroamerican culture to accept forgiveness, even when it is not asked for, is tantamount to admitting their complicity or guilt. Refusing to seek repentance is in fact a refusal to acknowledge that a moral debt is owed. Obviously, it is difficult, if not impossible, to offer individual forgiveness when neither regret nor remorse has been offered. Yet waiting for an oppressor to request forgiveness allows the dominant culture to keep the locus of power and reinforce its stranglehold on the marginalized. According to research conducted by psychologist Liz Gulliford, many who have offered forgiveness have reported a "profound sense of personal release," even when the offender has not asked to be forgiven. If maintaining bitterness, hatred, and resentment negatively endangers one's well-being, then forgiveness cannot be contingent on the dominant culture's repentance (2004, 85-86).

Moving toward reconciliation without repentance can still prove beneficial to the unrepentant. Jesus ate and associated with the sinners of his day, including tax collectors and prostitutes, without first asking them to repent, and by this act many recognized their own complicity with sin and came to salvation. They recommitted the rest of their lives to the reign of God and the establishment of justice. Of course, this does not mean that we should always enter into relationships with those who have caused us pain. At times this may be unadvisable as well as unsafe. Before an actual relationship can be established, those within the dominant culture must come to terms with their undue power and privilege and address their participation in oppressive structures. Until then, the marginalized can, out of pity, offer forgiveness for the intrinsic value it provides them. Those trapped in anger, hatred, and bitterness, can offer forgiveness so as to shake the dust off their feet, and leave repentance in God's hands.

Jesus gave this advice to his disciples in the Gospel of Matthew. If anyone would not hear their words, they were to leave and "shake off the dust from your feet. For truly it will be more bearable to the lands of Sodom and Gomorrah on Judgment Day than for [those people]" (Matt. 10:14-15). Although the next verse reminds that us we are but sheep among wolves, we have a God who will ultimately deal with the wolves. By remembering that judgment and accountability have an eschatological dimension, an accounting in the future, it becomes possible to let go and move on with confidence in a God who proclaims, "Vengeance is mine, I will repay" (Rom. 12:19). Revenge or retaliation is not the responsibility of the injured person. Jonah was right, God does judge. As Abraham concluded while negotiating for the lives of the wicked of Sodom and Gomorrah, "Will not the judge of all the earth judge justly?" (Gen. 18:25).

ESTABLISHING JUSTICE

In the words of the psalmist, "Mercy and truth have met, justice and peace have kissed" (Ps. 85:10). Indeed, reconciliation is the intersection of mercy with truth once wrongdoing is acknowledged. Reconciliation invites the presence of both justice and peace. As Pope Paul VI reminded us: "Justice will bring about peace. . . . If you want peace, work for justice."[5] Peace as *shalom* means more then simple harmony. The Hebrew concept of *shalom* connotes solidarity, well-being, and wholeness—in short, a glimpse of the nature of heaven. For *shalom* to have significance, it must become one with justice. Without justice, words such as forgiveness, love, and reconciliation are meaningless. The transformative thread running throughout scripture is humanity's hope of reconciling with God and with each other—hence the greatest commandment to love God and our neighbor as ourselves (Matt. 22:34-40). *Shalom* can bring about justice, and justice can, in turn, secure *shalom*.

It is impossible to return to a pristine past before the genocide of indigenous peoples or enslavement of others. Centuries of violence have irrevocably marked the marginalized, making the retrieval of their former identity inconceivable. Reconciliation cannot pave the way for a return to the past by eliminating disenfranchisement and converting all oppressors to the God of life. But reconciliation can birth a new creation. "If anyone is in Christ," according to St. Paul, "that one is a new creation, the old has passed away. Behold, all things have become new" (2 Cor

---

[5] Message of Pope Paul VI for the celebration of the Day of Peace, given at the Vatican, January 1, 1972.

5:17). But this new creation requires great effort; it will not come into being by itself. With the birth of any new creation, there is the pain of "groaning in labor"(Rom. 8:22-23). If pain and suffering are to be productive, the ultimate goal must be wholeness and liberation. We must rely on God's Spirit to help us in our weakness during this protracted birthing process. Attempts to avoid the pain that usually accomplishes the birthing of a new social order often replace the painful actions required to dismantle power and privilege with feelings of guilt and shame, which serve no useful function. Guilt over the plight of the disenfranchised is meaningless if it is not linked to praxis that can enable the coming into being of a new creation.

Because God is a God of new creations, goodness and new life can come from centuries of racism and ethnic discrimination. Wounds may persist, but they should not be allowed to fester and become gangrenous carriers of premature death for the marginalized. Just as Christ still carries the scars of the crucifixion upon his flesh, today's crucified people, those whose lives are offered up for the sins of racism and ethnic discrimination, still carry their wounds upon their bodies, the wounds of inadequate health care, unequal educational and employment opportunities, and the burdens of life lived in crime-ridden, impoverished neighborhoods. To establish justice and to foster reconciliation are to dismantle the discriminatory walls historically created by the dominant culture. In the words of James Cone, "God's reconciliation means destroying all forms of slavery and oppression in white America so that the people of color can affirm the authenticity of their political freedom" (1975, 236).

Paul's epistle to the Ephesians provides an excellent illustration of tearing down walls that separate by power and privilege. The temple in Jerusalem was constructed to segregate people by ethnicity, gender, and privilege. Gentiles could enter the outermost areas, but they were forbidden to enter the inner parts of the temple, primarily because of their ethnicity, on the penalty of death. Paul was nearly killed by a mob on the unfounded accusation that he brought "Greeks into the temple" (Acts 21:27-29). Beyond the space created for Gentiles to worship the living God was the Women's Court, which, as the name implies, was an area

Jewish women were allowed to enter, but they could go no farther. The next area, known as the Court of Israel, was a space
constructed only for Jewish men. Beyond that, the Priest's Court
was reserved for the priests. The final court of exclusion was
called the Holy of Holies and only the high priest could enter this
space to encounter the presence of God. Closeness to the presence of God was clearly dependent on privilege and power.

Ephesians tells us that the coming of Jesus has dismantled this
hierarchy. Speaking to the Gentiles, those who were historically
segregated, Paul reminded his audience of the time when they
were excluded from membership in the people of God. "For
Christ is the peace between us," writes Paul, "He has made the
two of us into one, breaking down the middle walls of partitions
which used to keep us apart, actually annulling in his own flesh
the hostility caused by commandments and decrees of the Law"
(2:14-15). Jesus Christ provides *shalom*. He has torn down the
walls of the temple so that everyone, regardless of ethnicity, race,
or gender, can walk with confidence into the Holy of Holies, the
very presence of God.

Restorative and Retributive Justice

Any reconciliation process must include providing material
and psychological support for those who continue to be marginalized. There must be a concerted effort to move away from either
conservative or liberal guilt, a guilt that elicits apologies while
refusing to tamper with self-perpetuating structures that create
and award privilege. Failure to radically change the existing
power structures to bring about justice only undermines society's
ability to live under any future system of agreed rules. We can
move beyond guilt and political correctness toward actual reconciliation only when we move beyond retributive justice—the
form of justice with a strong component of punishment sought by
Jonah—to restorative justice.

Although the focus of marginalized communities should
remain on restorative justice, retribution should not be totally
overlooked. This does not mean the implementation of the *lex
talionis*, which limits vengeance by imposing justice as "an eye

for an eye, tooth for a tooth." True, the goal of God's justice, as ethicist John De Gruchy reminds us, is "healing and reconciliation . . . [a] justice of restored relations" (2002, 201-2). But restorative justice must include a retributional component. Retribution is not a call to exact revenge; it is a call for justice. Such justice, as Robert J. Schreiter reminds us, "is a symbolic act that admits that a full and complete justice cannot be done: the dead cannot be brought back, or health may never be fully restored. It represents, however, an act on the part of the new [social order] to make amends in some measure for the harm that has been inflicted" (1998, 122). And generations of discrimination have inflicted harm. Restitution is required for the spiritually and physically impoverishing effects institutionalized violence has had on the disenfranchised.

John De Gruchy is correct in pointing out that "the pursuit of social justice [is] the only antidote to vengeance" (2002, 123). Still, it is important not to confuse retribution with vengeance. Communal forgiveness neither rules out state-sponsored retribution for offenders nor restitution for those victimized. Justice must restore the full humanity of those seen and treated as objects throughout multiple generations, and punishment may be needed to hold oppressors accountable. A nonvengeful response to wrongdoers, a response that rejects punitive justice as synonymous with revenge, is what Donald Shriver calls "just punishment" (2001, 157). And while individuals or marginalized communities wishing to remain faithful to the gospel message are not called to exact retribution, society as a whole must hold oppressors accountable by connecting repentance with restitution. In his letter to the Romans, Paul reminds us that the role of governmental authorities is to "serve God. They carry out God's vengeance by punishing wrongdoers" (13:4). Again, the emphasis of restorative justice should never rest solely on punishing wrongdoers; the focus must always remain on restoring the marginalized by dismantling structures that normalize and legitimize racial and ethnic discrimination.

Latin American theologian José Comblin reminds us that reconciliation and liberation are not an either-or proposition. Liberation from oppressive structures or the restoration of human dignity is required before communal forgiveness can be offered. If the present structures that continue to privilege white supremacy are not first dismantled, reconciliation cannot take place (1986, 272-314). The focus of communal forgiveness must be on ushering in social and economic justice, and such a focus can very well mean a redistribution of wealth and power. In effect, the power and privilege of the dominant culture must be nailed to the cross and crucified with Jesus before any discussion of communal forgiveness can take place. Put simply, without justice there is no peace; without peace there is no justice nor hope for reconciliation.

The path to justice and reconciliation is not an easy path to walk. Past atrocities will always have a legacy. The spirits of generations of ancestors who have suffered under racial and ethnic discrimination may not fully be pacified until the time of God's final judgment. Indeed, the Book of Revelation provides an image of all those unjustly killed on account of God's word before the altar of heaven, crying out, "Holy and true Master, how much longer will you wait before you judge and take vengeance for our blood on those dwelling on the earth?" (6:9-11). It is impossible to compensate for the centuries of stolen labor, broken bodies, and lost opportunities, all because God created many peoples as nonwhite. Or, as Nigel Walker, a criminology professor at Cambridge University, so eloquently puts it: "Victims can be compensated, but not unraped or unmugged" (Biggar 2003, 10-11). Even if some consensus existed that those who continue to rape and mug through economic means should somehow be held accountable, our political structures would never allow this nation's elite to stand trial for all they "legally" appropriated from marginalized communities.

DECIDING FOR COMMUNAL FORGIVENESS

Communal forgiveness is the decision of the whole not to seek revenge, a decision that leads toward, and is also the product of, reconciliation. But forgiveness cannot unite a disjointed community until the dominant culture deals with the injustices that con-

tinue to create the powerful and the powerless. Communal forgiveness that is substituted for justice makes a mockery of both.
There can be no communal forgiveness without a profound
realignment of how power operates in society. For this reason,
while the dominant culture may continue to crave communal forgiveness, it is most unwilling to alter the present power structures.
While individual forgiveness can be a unilateral act to bring healing to the victim and possible redemption to the victimizer who
benefits, communal forgiveness can occur only within a relationship based on justice and equality. Arriving at communal forgiveness can be an arduous task, a task that may need to engage
generations.

In spite of the fact that some wrongs exist that can never be
corrected, communal forgiveness does open wide a door by providing an opportunity for the privileged and the marginalized to
come together to work for justice. As such, it becomes a grace
given by the marginalized and not something earned or
demanded by the dominant culture. The process that can lead to
communal forgiveness requires listening as a community to the
stories that arise from the margins. More than likely, because of
the dominant culture's resistance to hearing these stories, they
need to be told over and over and over again until new possibilities become evident. Through accounts of the historical and present truth, the dominant culture can begin to understand its
complicity with oppressive structures. Even more important, as
the marginalized tell their stories, they cease being passive objects
of the dominant culture. In the telling of their stories, they gain
subjectivity and agency, vital components of their humanity.
Reclaiming their humanity, then, requires recognition of that
humanity by the dominant culture, a group more accustomed to
looking past or dismissing persons at the margins.

All too often, when members of the dominant culture are confronted with their complicity with structures of oppression, they
either begin to see themselves as the ones being victimized or they
develop the argument that we are all victims. In one particular
class I taught on marginalized communities, one white woman
stated that she too was oppressed because she was left-handed in
a classroom where all the chairs are for right-handed people.

Although I had no desire to minimize the insensitivity of right-handed administrators who purchased only right-handed chairs, nor the inconvenience this created for our left-handed students, her experience fell far short of the past and present-day experiences of people of color.

A student in another class stated loudly that because he was a white male, he was the one who was truly oppressed in this age of political correctness. Robert H. Bork, the neoconservative legal jurist nominated to the U.S. Supreme Court but not confirmed by Congress, once maintained that the only group that is truly oppressed in the United States today is white, heterosexual males. He accused people of color of participating in a rhetoric of victimhood so as to force Euroamericans to seek absolution from those they have supposedly oppressed (1996, 228-29). Recasting those with power as victims is an attempt to short-circuit any endeavor to restructure society in order to protect and secure privilege.

Progress toward communal forgiveness to bring about reconciliation can never move forward until the dominant culture abandons its profession of innocence. This is why communal forgiveness must begin at the margins of society, where false professions of innocence are identified as sins of power.

CONCLUSION

Some members of the dominant culture understand forgiveness and reconciliation as interchangeable concepts. Others propose a formula *reconciliation → forgiveness → repentance*. They argue that when the marginalized reconcile and forgive their oppressors, then those privileged by the present social structures will be led to repentance. For them, reconciliation is contingent neither on their repentance nor on their implementation of justice. In this model, reconciliation does not come about because the marginalized have not forgiven their oppressors.

Although the model for establishing a reconciled community advocated within the dominant culture may sound doable in theory, it naively ignores how power works, specifically how those in power never willingly relinquish their power; forgiveness offered by the disenfranchised makes little difference to them. In the final analysis, if the dominant culture is truly to seek reconciliation, it risks losing its privileged space in society. Indeed, the only viable model for reconciliation is a model that remains focused on those victimized by the present power structures. Such a model is a process of steps moving from *rebuke* to *personal forgiveness*, then *repentance, justice, communal forgiveness*, and, finally, *reconciliation*.

Jonah did a superb job with the first step—rebuke. And although he may have felt pleased with verbally lashing out at his sworn enemies, one is left to wonder what might have been if Jonah had set aside his personal feelings and attempted to offer personal forgiveness? Would the Assyrians still have repented? If so, would they have understood why they needed to repent? Obviously we cannot relive the past. Still, we are left wondering, and even hoping, that if Jonah had been more proactive he might have brought about reconciliation between Assyria and Israel, and perhaps even averted the eventual decimation of his nation by the Assyrians.

5

Pitfalls Jonah Should Avoid

JONAH WAS CALLED to be an evangelist, but his call was not that of today's evangelists. Nowadays, we use the term "evangelist" to refer to certain individuals who attempt to convince "nonbelievers" to believe the doctrinal suppositions held by the evangelist. Today's evangelists seem to be heirs to the great missionary enterprise that was part of the colonization process. Then, and also now, religious doctrine and cultural norms were so interconnected that it was difficult, if not impossible, to differentiate Christianity from the Euroamerican culture in which it was embedded. Evangelism described a process by which "heathens" became like "us"—like the British or the French or the Spanish, or later on, the Euroamericans. Such a definition was at best faulty, at worst destructive. The "white man's burden" of Christianizing and civilizing the pagans was a process pregnant with the prejudice and paternalism of racial superiority—a process responsible for cultural, if not physical, genocide. It is not surprising that the voices of the world's marginalized rejected this form of evangelism.

American history has seen other waves of evangelists, from the founding of the Protestant empire in the American colonies in the seventeenth century, through the revivals of the nineteenth and twentieth centuries, to the televangelists of the present time. My interest in evangelism is somewhat different and more in tune with Jonah's efforts in Nineveh. The normative understanding of Jonah is that of a somewhat failed evangelist, someone called to preach God's message of repentance to heathens so that they might be saved. But as we have seen in the earlier chapters, the story of Jonah can also be understood as the story of a person from the margins calling the Assyrian powers to reconciliation. In reality, Jonah's call to evangelize the Assyrians was a mission to convince a people of their humanity, even though they were guilty of inhuman acts. Oppression creates inhuman conditions not only for the oppressed but also for the oppressors; those who benefit from these conditions also lose their humanity in the process. Not only are salvation and liberation for the oppressed; they are also for the oppressors. In a very real sense, to evangelize is to work toward reconciliation in the relationship between God and human beings, between human beings, and between human beings and creation. But, as already noted, evangelizing those in power, particularly if they are already Christians, serves no real purpose if repentance is absent. Even Jesus stressed this point.

> This is an evil generation for it seeks a sign, but a sign will not be given to it, except the sign of the prophet Jonah. Just as Jonah was a sign to the Ninevites, so too will the Son be a sign for this generation. . . . Ninevites will rise up on the judgment day and will condemn this generation because they repented at the preaching of Jonah. And behold, a greater than Jonah is here. (Luke 11:29-30, 32)

Fostering reconciliation requires repentance by the dominant culture. To evangelize is to confront the dominant culture with its sins of privilege and power, which is responsible for much of the plight of the world's disenfranchised.

The work of liberation and reconciliation is an evangelical project to which the marginalized, like Jonah, are called. Such an evangelism is fraught with pitfalls. This chapter will explore some of these pitfalls, fully aware that this is not an exhaustive list, but also fully aware of the need to move forward, to take some concrete steps.

WHOSE DEFINITIONS?

Obstacles and concerns do exist for those trying to bring about reconciliation. Probably the most glaring pitfall, as we have seen, is that the entire discourse on reconciliation is embedded within a Eurocentric construction of what reconciliation means. Christians seeking reconciliation are usually so entrapped and enmeshed in their culture that Euroamerican Christians, from either the fundamentalist right or the far liberal left, probably have more in common with each other and understand each other better than they do Christians on the other side of the racial and ethnic divide. Presentations and writings of religious leaders associated with either the religious right or the religious left demonstrate their beliefs in the Euroamerican process—although they agree that some reforms may still be needed—and a lack of understanding or a *mis*understanding of what it means to reside on the margins of society. Hope and salvation still form a Eurocentric project deeply rooted in the "American way."

The divide between the privileged and the disenfranchised— those who believe in the "American way" and those who have never shared in the "American dream"—is manifested in how ethics is understood and practiced. On the margins of society, ethics focuses on the communal. By contrast, in most Eurocentric churches the focus remains primarily on personal piety, although some exceptions may exist among those churches with strong social justice programs. When did churchgoers last hear a sermon on corporate sin or corporate responsibility? Most sermons stress how we as individuals fall short of God's glory, or how we as individuals can come closer to God's ideal. Not surprisingly, many sermons are based on how to pray more effectively, tithe more, or overcome individual temptations.

So why do churches avoid challenging the empire? We have already explored some of the possibilities, mainly how the church is embedded in the prevailing social structures. To begin with, the success of the empire, the financial security of churches, and those with privilege and power are connected. Many church portfolios and individual retirement accounts depend on the success of multinational corporations. Pensions, increases in endowments, and other forms of economic survival depend on the increasing value of financial investments. Advocating issues of justice such as a living wage, environmental responsibility, or safety regulations could have a negative impact on profit and directly affect dividends paid to shareholders, including both church portfolios and those who give to churches. The economic survival or success of many U.S. Christians and their houses of worship is tied to the success of the neoliberal economic system.

Just as economic benefits have been privatized through the stock market, so too have the concepts of forgiveness and reconciliation been confined to the realm of personal piety. For most Christians, reconciliation has been reduced to a confessional process that seeks from God, through Christ, the forgiveness of individual sins. Any positive consequences to interpersonal relations, while welcomed, are probably limited to interactions between a few individuals. For all practical purposes, reconciliation has ceased being a communal process, becoming more a matter of what Jesus can do "for me." Similarly, "Jesus saves" means Jesus saves *me*. While I do not wish to minimize the importance of personal faith, such faith lacks substance if it solely imitates the individualism of our culture. Reconciliation with God, whom we cannot see, is an illusion if reconciliation with our sisters and brothers whom we can see is not included.

Reconciliation from the margins of society could take quite a different turn. The margins could prophetically call the church to bring about reconciliation—not just with God but also with creation, between different communities and within communities as well as with other persons. Nevertheless, the Christian church, as a human institution, remains a social construct embedded in the power structures of the overall culture. Fortunately, the movement of God, through God's Spirit, can work for reconciliation within and through the church in spite of its being a social construct. But Christian churches must remain centered on the gospel message, which includes the immensity of crucifying sin and the call to forge solidarity with the "least of these." This is the Christian path to salvation.

How does the Spirit move in churches that focus on preserving their exalted positions in the overall culture? How can real societal change come about when churches continue to employ their ties to cultural and economic power structures that limit the capacities for abundant life for all people? Efforts toward reconciliation in such Spirit-void churches ignore the lived experience of marginalized communities. While grandiose pronouncements may be made on Martin Luther King Day against the evils of racism and ethnic discrimination, changes in such churches rarely come about. Confessions of sins that prevent reconciliation are meaningless unless a church is actively involved in dismantling the very social structures designed to provide it with privilege. *Only by losing its privileged space in the culture can the church hope to gain a place at God's table.* Church as community requires not just individual confessions of sins but communal confessions of complicity in the sins of oppression and injustice. While individual pleas for forgiveness are important, even more important in bringing about real change in the world is corporate penitence that commits to letting "justice roll down like waters, and righteousness like an ever-flowing stream" (Amos 5:24).

Is it any wonder that those in the dominant culture and those in marginalized communities of color end up talking past one another? Forgiveness and reconciliation are understood differently. If the dominant culture is allowed to define reconciliation, then those privileged by the status quo establish the parameters of discussion and actions; they also determine when the goal of reconciliation has been achieved. Even when intentions are noble, the privileged cannot escape a culture that has reimagined a past to portray a history that is basically good, although occasionally misguided. Popular media, history books, political pronouncements, and a general amnesia silence the voices of those existing on the underside of U.S. progress. When their story is ignored, forgotten, romanticized, and/or distorted, there is no need for reconciliation.

The world witnessed a sudden and basically unwelcome unveiling of racial discrimination and poverty during the aftermath of New Orleans' devastation caused by Hurricane Katrina. Thousands of U.S. citizens who were black and poor were abandoned as a direct result of a national policy that continues to reward the richest segments of society through tax cuts under the philosophy that "a rising tide lifts all boats." Although Michael Chertoff, the homeland security secretary, told National Public Radio that he had "not heard a report of thousands of people in the convention center who don't have food and water," the rest of America and the world saw the twenty-five thousand stranded citizens on television a full day before the man responsible heard of their distress.[1] What our television sets showed us is that the "boats" that left New Orleans with the high tide were piloted by and for the privileged of society. Those who had no boats, mostly black, mostly poor, were left behind to their fate. Even when the cavalry finally showed up, it first evacuated the seven hundred guests and employees at the Hyatt Hotel before turning to the city's residents, proving once again that class and white privilege have their "perks."

Barbara Bush, mother of the president during the Katrina disaster and wife of a former president, best revealed the pitfall of allowing the dominant Euroamerican culture to define the situation and experience of people of color. While touring the Houston Astrodome with her husband, former president George H. W. Bush, and former president Bill Clinton, Barbara Bush explained the situation of thousands of Hurricane Katrina victims huddled on their government-issued green army cots. The former first lady basically said that they did not have it so bad because, after all, they were poor to begin with. "What I'm hearing, which is sort of scary, is they all want to stay in Texas," she was quoted as saying in an interview with National Public Radio. "Everyone is so overwhelmed by the hospitality, and so many of the people in the arena here, you know, were underprivileged anyway, so this is working very well for them."[2] It is only the powerful and privileged who see handouts, rather than justice, as "working very well."

CONSEQUENCES OF CHALLENGING WHITE PRIVILEGE

Additional pitfalls are, first, that reconciliation with the marginalized poses a threat to white hegemony, and second, that his-

---

[1] Frank Rich, "Falluja Floods the Superdome," *New York Times*, September 4, 2005.

[2] Angela Rozas, "Barbara Bush's Remark Clarified," *Chicago Tribune*, September 8, 2005.

tory provides few, if any, examples of those with power willingly relinquishing power to the disenfranchised. Reducing reconciliation to the private sphere maintains white hegemony by allowing the dominant culture to ignore the plight of marginalized communities of color, even as it celebrates multiculturalism. Many celebrations of multiculturalism designed to prove that racism has indeed been conquered seem no more than empty statements of political correctness. Validations of the cultural symbols of the oppressed can include white choirs singing gospel or bilingual hymns or the inclusion of prayers in Spanish or Korean; on occasion congregations may even relent and allow drums during a worship service. Multiculturalism is encouraged as long as white church leadership is not challenged. But authentic multiculturalism must go beyond warm fuzzy feelings toward other cultures to actually questioning or changing how power operates. Emphasizing personal piety, what an individual must do to find peace with a particular brother or sister of color, although desirable, does not go far enough.

If reconciliation is reduced to a multiculturalism of symbolic concessions, change cannot take place. One of the major tenets of the civil rights movement was the need for a redistribution of wealth. Instead, the dominant culture of elected representatives reduced the movement to voting rights. Voting rights are important and are a worthy goal, but redistribution of wealth would have struck at the heart of white hegemony. Victory in the struggle for civil rights was declared by white America when the Civil Rights Act of 1964 was passed, but the basic structures supporting white supremacy remained unchanged. Any praxis leading to true reconciliation must be consciousness-raising and must move far beyond the symbolic level.

Storytelling can be an effective tool to move reconciliation beyond abstract or theoretical discussions toward praxis. As South African ethicist John de Gruchy reminds us, "the best way to speak about reconciliation is through story-telling rather than through systematic expositions of dogma" (2002, 22). Telling stories from the past is often avoided by the dominant culture because the stories can challenge their collective memory. Stories that immediately come to mind include accounts of how several in the Cherokee Nation in the early nineteenth century adopted the religion, agricultural practices, and lifestyles of whites in order to assimilate and coexist, only to be forced in the 1830s on an eight-hundred-mile journey known as the Trails of Tears, which took them far from their homelands. About a quarter of the Cherokee nation perished during this trek. Or how white mobs systematically attacked and brutally killed Chinese laborers in the late nineteenth century throughout the West because they were viewed as competition for low-paying jobs. Or how in the early twentieth century Texans knew when the Texas Rangers rode through by the number of Mexicans left behind, hanging from trees, shot in the back of the head, or bodies discarded after being dragged behind the Rangers' horses.

Those with privilege are rarely willing to admit that they have benefited from past and present injustices, an inconvenient fact easily skipped over in a rush to embrace symbolic gestures of reconciliation. Storytelling can serve as a check to the temptation to hurry over stories of pain and suffering caused by disenfranchisement in order to find solutions. While reconciliation may still be found someplace in the distant future, the telling of stories becomes an important step to building bridges by fostering empathy for those who suffered. While finding solutions is crucial and should never be underestimated, listening to stories must be the first step in the praxis of reconciliation.

The telling and hearing of stories can be facilitated by a truth-commission model, as used in countries that have experienced social conflict and violence. Through a truth-commission model, current stories of disenfranchisement can be connected to past U.S. atrocities and violations. Ethicist Audrey R. Chapman notes:

> A truth commission's purpose is to provide a narrative of a specific period and/or regime, determine the major causes of the violence, and recommend measures to undertake so as to avoid a repetition in the future. Once victims' accounts are verified, official acknowledgment of abuse can support the credibility of their suffering and help restore their dignity. (2001, 258-59)

The lack of a format for a national discussion of abuse and oppression, such as a truth commission, impedes the United States from actively participating in the sharing of stories. The inability to hear stories from the margins of power and privilege leads the dominant Euroamerican culture to what are often misguided ways of trying to bring about reconciliation.

A basic obstacle to the process of reconciliation is the conviction, often accompanied by near arrogance, of members of the dominant culture that they are the "fixers," that *they* are able to bring about reconciliation. They do not realize that they themselves are subject to the political and cultural power structures that privilege them. For this reason, achieving reconciliation is never easy and seldom straightforward. If the privileged within the dominant culture benefit from the present structures and thus have power, why can't they just simply change the structures? Why can't they just fix it? Regardless of the level or passion of their commitment to justice and reconciliation, the existing structures will work against their desires in order to protect their interests. Members of the privileged class are not completely free agents, because they too are subject to the existing structures. The structures that privilege them are also designed to prevent them from changing the flow of privilege. And thus the aphorism, "It's hard to work against the system."

THE PITFALLS OF POWER

This leads to a third pitfall—underestimating power. Any attempt to foster a reconciled and just community in the United States is bound to fail if it does not give serious consideration to the power of the neoliberal economy, the power of entrenched racism and ethnic discrimination embedded in our social structures, and the power that Constantinian Christians have in the political process. Michel Foucault may be correct in observing that the power residing in the dominant culture, like truth, is a construct produced "by multiple forms of constraint" (1980, 131). In other words, the social location of those privileged by society profoundly shapes and forms their beliefs, practices, and even their definitions of reality—in effect, the truths of their world. Even though Foucault insists that truth is not revealed or discovered but rather *produced*, there exists an uneasiness within marginalized communities about forsaking the existence of the truth of their marginalization. Those who are marginalized know that something is wrong with how the social order functions, while those with power and privilege are sheltered from what the marginalized experience on a daily basis. Marginality places the oppressed in a better position to grasp the truth of the present reality. Unlike the privileged, they must know how to survive in the world of power and privilege as well as live in their own world. There is no need for the privileged to know anything about what it means to be disenfranchised. In effect, the marginalized better understand the truth of their reality than those residing in communities of privilege. Although Jesus proclaimed that the truth will set us free (John 8:32), the Euroamerican culture remains trapped in the bondage of falsehood while it protects its misappropriated privilege and power. Power produces meaning for the dominant culture, including the normative meaning of terms such as "justice" or "reconciliation."

Political and economic supremacy often produces the notions of spiritual supremacy, so that those privileged by the social structures also see themselves as the guardians and definers of ethics and morality. Definitions of justice and reconciliation put forth by the dominant culture are inherently oppressive because they consciously or unconsciously preserve their privilege. Whatever is harmful to their privileged space is in their minds harmful for the entire culture and thus wrong or immoral in and of itself. To bring about real change, definitions of justice and reconciliation created by the dominant culture for the dominant culture must be discarded.

Still, we must refuse to accept a simplistic dichotomy that those from the dominant culture are "bad" while those found on the underside are "good." Such a dichotomy serves no purpose other than creating a sense of guilt among the predominantly white class of the privileged and a sense of entitlement among people of color. Another concern to keep in mind is the difficulty faced by members of the dominant culture who want to bring about justice only to face overwhelming structures designed to perpetuate the status quo. Guilt combined with frustration leads to inactivity on the part of well-intentioned Christians. The end result is often that the dominant culture is uncomfortable with even mentioning race or with being among people of color because of their need to prove that they are not racist.

Shedding tears over present injustices all too often becomes a substitute for the rigors of attempting to understand how power actually works to bestow privilege. No one questions that those who benefit from white supremacy should feel guilty. Nevertheless, the margins of society gain nothing and do not need the tears of white guilt; marginalized communities have shed enough tears for both themselves and the dominant culture. What the disenfranchised need from the dominant culture is concrete praxis that will begin to dismantle systems of privilege. Tears accomplish little, except for those with power who experience a "healing" or cleansing, which provides no benefits for the marginalized.

Even strong allies of disenfranchised communities, regardless of their courageous stands taken in the past, can easily revert back to taking advantage of their privilege. The apostle Peter is a good example. With his commitment to a multicultural church, Peter was the first believer in the risen Christ to visit the home of an "unclean" Gentile and bring him and his family the good news, an act for which he was criticized and forced to defend himself before the Christian church leaders (Acts 10:1–11:18). Although Peter was responsible for opening the church's doors to all, including the Gentiles, he is the same Peter who, while visiting Antioch some time later, refused to eat with Gentiles out of fear of how others might view him (Gal. 2:11-14). Even when a decision is made to walk in solidarity with the oppressed, those from the Euroamerican dominant culture always have the option of returning to their privilege whenever it suits their needs. Courage and faithfulness are required from those wishing to accompany the marginalized.

The only time members of the dominant culture can participate in solidarity with racially and marginalized communities to pursue justice and reconciliation is when they are willing to engage in self-negation; they must nail their sins of white and class privilege to the cross so that justice can freely flow. Self-negation does not come easily. Friedrich Nietzsche labeled this mind-set a life-denying "slave morality," which he contrasted with a "master morality." A "master morality" would view the offering of forgiveness as a weak virtue that would only encourage repetition of the offense that required forgiveness in the first place. Offering forgiveness would only reinforce the inferiority of marginalized groups who lack the courage and self-respect to fight for their rights. Nevertheless, any engagement in the work of reconciliation demands a rejection of master morality and the embracing of a so-called slave morality—an act that by its very nature can be achieved only by dismantling the power and privilege of the dominant culture.

Any attempts to dismantle the power base of the dominant culture must also consider seriously whether or not or how they might negatively impact the disenfranchised. A significant component of privilege is not having to be conscious of one's identity through race or ethnicity. Theologian Thandeka creates what she terms the "race game" to demonstrate how whites have difficulty seeing their skin color. She asked Euroamericans to add the word "white" when describing a person who is also Euroamerican, as in "my white friend," "my white teacher," or "my white co-worker," similar to the way they use color or ethnicity to describe members of marginalized communities. What the "game" revealed is that while Euroamericans have no difficulty saying, "my black friend," "my Hispanic teacher," or "my Asian co-worker," they could not bring themselves to name their own race. In their minds, whiteness is normative and thus would be redundant (1999, 3-5).

Despite the abundance today of color-blind rhetoric, those in marginalized communities of color are never allowed to forget that they fall short of the normative white ideal. Not a day goes by that people of color are not made aware that they really do not belong. Discovering that one is different can occur in shocking and painful ways. Daryl Davis, a young boy living in Massachusetts in the 1960s, discovered his black race when he joined the

Cub Scouts. One day, all the scouting groups in the area were invited to march in commemoration of Paul Revere's famous ride. Davis marched, oblivious to the fact that he was the only black Scout. Not long into the march, he began to be pelted with rocks and other flying objects. At first he naively thought that the spectators lining the parade route hated Cub Scouts. It wasn't until the Cub Master and Den Mother ran to walk beside him, thus shielding him with their own bodies that Davis realized that he was the only Scout to be attacked. That day, Davis learned what it meant to be black (Davis 1998, 4).

Reconciliation cannot be effectively discussed without first considering the construction of identity. Dominant cultures always require an "Other": for some to be "in" or "on top," others must be "out" or "below." Defining the racially and ethnically marginalized persons as inferior, first culturally and then morally, allows members of the dominant culture to see themselves through the process of negation: they are morally and spiritually superior because they are *not* like their black, brown, red, or yellow Others. This represents a serious danger for members of disenfranchised communities, who then begin to see themselves through the eyes of the dominant culture, even though the members of that group profess color blindness and claim not to see race. For persons of color and disenfranchisement that may have perdured for generations, it is a matter of time before they start to define themselves through the images flickering on the screens of theaters or the television sets in their living rooms. As popular media reinforce the negative stereotypes of racial and ethnically diverse groups, a sense of inferiority and worthlessness develops. The marginalized of color begin to compare their situation with those of the dominant culture and put the blame on themselves and their own diminished skills. This can easily lead to a sense of helplessness and an inability to determine one's own destiny. If they are unable to help themselves, who will provide salvation?

Here lies the crux of the problem. Members of marginalized racial and ethnic communities often shape themselves in the image of the dominant culture; they learn to mimic the attitudes, beliefs, behaviors, and actions that they have been taught to see as superior. This is a form of colonization of the mind, in which the marginalized learn their "lack of self-worth" and experience self-loathing. Some marginalized persons seem to attempt to become "whiter" than the dominant culture. If salvation requires assimilation—at least in terms of the dominant culture—then proof of worthiness lies in being accepted by the dominant culture, even if this leads to actions that are contrary or damning to one's own community of color.

No doubt some in marginalized communities obtain "the American dream," or believe they have. But this does not vindicate assimilation. Class privilege does create opportunities for some in marginalized groups to participate and benefit from the existing power structures. This is a danger, however, when at times those who have unexpectedly gained privilege exhibit greater disdain and less patience or compassion than their white counterparts for those in their own communities who fall short of the white ideal, usually persons who are darker and poorer. When the marginalized who vocally support the many manifestation of white supremacy are lifted onto pedestals, the message to racial and ethnic communities is clear: if you also want to succeed, then emulate these success stories. You too can become "a credit to your race." The lure of economic privilege has a way of seducing everyone, including those in marginalized groups, to seek benefits for themselves instead of justice for all. Two decades ago, Alice Walker questioned some of the consequences of the civil rights movement, lamenting:

> I think Medger Evers and Martin Luther King, Jr., would be dismayed by the lack of radicalism in the new black middle class, and discouraged to know that a majority of the black people helped by the Movement of the sixties has abandoned itself to the pursuit of cars, expensive furniture, large houses, and the finest Scotch. (1984, 168)

Commenting on Alice Walker, Alistair Kee succinctly probed to the heart of the matter: "Political emancipation is not human emancipation" (2005, 49). If the "pursuit of cars, expensive furniture, large houses, and the finest Scotch" can be achieved only by learning to play along with oppressive structures, this is a terribly high price to pay by those in marginalized communities. Then they become apologists for the present systems of injustice. It is not surprising that the dominant culture offers lucrative rewards to such spokespersons. Prominent examples are Linda Chavez, a Latina who was tapped to head the Center for Equal Opportunity, or Ward Connerly, an African American who heads the Center for Individual Rights—two organizations that served at the forefront in defending the suit of white plaintiffs against the University of Michigan affirmative action policies in 2004 and 2005.

Individuals like Linda Chavez and Ward Connerly remind us that the need for reconciliation goes beyond the dominant culture and historically U.S. marginalized communities. The lure of becoming new oppressors at the expense of other marginalized groups is a reality that finds expression in various forms of oppression within such communities, such as internal racism, sexism, and classism, where proximity to the white male ideal remains the standard for measuring superiority. The closer one is to the white ideal, the more privilege exists—although still limited within the overall dominant culture. Reconciliation is also needed among the disenfranchised where oppressive structures also exist. It is easy to detect the sins that the dominant culture perpetrates against our marginalized communities, and while these oppressive structures should never be minimized, it is also important to be aware of and active in dismantling the ways we emulate the dominant culture in oppressing segments in our own communities. Surely God stands against all oppression, even that perpetrated by the oppressed.

Any decision to find salvation through assimilation is difficult to unpack. Obviously, individual motives are always complex. Exploring human relationships, educator Paulo Freire noted that everyone in some part of their being seeks to be a "subject" who is able to act and transform her or his environment. Thus, members of marginalized communities who are objects acted upon, rather than subjects who do the acting, have an escape route. While habitually alienated and acted upon, they desire acceptance and want to become subjects in their own right. The safe route is to imitate the dominant society whose acceptance they crave. In a very real sense, their consciousness becomes submerged; they become unable, or unwilling, to see how they have internalized the operating interests and values of the dominant culture (1994, 25-30).

Although some from marginalized communities may attempt to join the dominant culture in order to share partially in the spoils of privilege, others among the disenfranchised refuse to resist oppressive structures for the sake of survival or the desire to protect loved ones. As political scientist James C. Scott points out:

> A cruel paradox of slavery, for example, is that it is in the interest of slave mothers, whose overriding wish is to keep their children safe and by their side, to train them in the routines of conformity. Out of love, they undertake to socialize their children to please, or at least not anger, their master and mistresses. (1990, 24)

And while we no longer live under a slavocracy, still, the principle of conformity to survive is a reality that can be attested to by the working poor in communities of color; some must learn to keep their mouths shut and avoid political actions lest they find themselves without the means to feed their families. Womanist ethicist Katie Cannon recalls the advice of her mother: "When you have your head in the lion's mouth, you have to treat the lion very gently" (Cannon and Heyward 1994, 61). New Testament scholar Anthony Bash and psychologist Melanie Bash describe another way that a lack of power can restrain the disenfranchised from moving toward reconciliation:

> A person who has been wronged may feel powerless because abused. In forgiving, the wronged person gives up their defenses against the abuse, such as anger or self-pity. Forgiveness may mean the wronged person acknowledges their powerlessness, and the pain and suffering of being wronged. It may also mean that the wronged person gives up the hope

of having the pain and suffering acknowledged in some way. (2004, 45)

Finally, we cannot ignore the power structures existing within our own marginalized communities that cause injustice and require exposure and dismantling. Jonah may have traveled to Nineveh to proclaim God's word against the oppression of the Israelite people, but he seems to have ignored the unjust rule of his own king, Jeroboam II, who, according to the Bible, "did evil in the eyes of YHWH and did not turn aside from all the sins of Jeroboam son of Nebat" (2 Kgs. 14:24). It is crucial to recognize that oppressive structures also exist within and between marginalized communities and they also demand attention. Domination exists within domination, and there are even margins within the margins. We should not deny that many communities of color can be as sexist, homophobic, classist, and racist (based on who is closer to the white ideal) as the dominant culture.

Centuries of powerlessness to dialogue or deal as equals with the dominant Euroamerican culture has at times led some in marginalized communities to turn what little energies exist into oppressing others in their communities, even though they are emulating the very structures that were used to disenfranchise them in the first place. Even within the margins it is possible to carve out spaces in which relative power and privilege can be achieved. Power brokers in communities of color may benefit from the status quo of white supremacy because their own power, limited though it may be, is contingent on maintaining things as they are. As communities of color strive for liberation and reconciliation focusing on dismantling oppressive structures of racism and ethnic discrimination that benefit the dominant culture, they must also actively engage in dismantling such structures within their own communities, particularly those of racism, sexism, classism, and heterosexism. As theologian Miroslav Volf noted, this is the revolutionary character of Jesus's proclamation that makes the "connection between the hope he gives to the oppressed and the radical change he requires of them" (1996, 114).

All too often, the more marginalized within disenfranchised communities (usually darker, usually female, and often homosexual) are told to remain quiet for now while the community presents a united voice to the dominant culture. Still, it can be dangerous for marginalized communities to discard internal reconciliation in favor of communal unity. If history is any guide, the concerns of the weakest within a disenfranchised community will likely not be addressed, even while progress may be taking place on reconciliation with the dominant culture.

SEEKING PEACE

Another pitfall to avoid is confusing reconciliation with peace. To seek reconciliation is, in a very real sense, to seek conflict, strife, and even violence. As long as reconciliation remains a noun, calls for repentance, as important as they are, can easily be ignored by the dominant culture. Reconciliation needs to become a verb that describes the act of moving from injustice toward justice. The absence of strife is neither peace nor reconciliation; it can simply be a truce. We all know of couples or families who never fight, yet a coldness is present instead of a feeling of warmth and intimacy. The same is true with communities. Seeking peace at all costs can lead to a very unjust justice. The goal should be not peace but rather a striving toward reconciliation that, if successful, will first cause upheavals and trials. In the words of Jesus in the Gospel of Matthew, "Do not think that I came to bring peace on the earth, not peace but the sword" (Matt. 10:34). Because justice never flows freely from oppressors, conflict will be a natural consequence in any struggle for reconciliation.

For most of its existence since the time of Constantine, the church has contributed to fostering injustices. The historical complicity of the church with empire and the injustice of empire have often prevented the dominant Christian community from acting as an agent of the moral change of reconciliation. Ideally, the church's role should be to overcome any alienation experienced by people of color and other disenfranchised groups caused by the prevailing injustices within society by establishing a peace based on justice. As Volf points out, "Churches, the presumed agents of reconciliation, are at best impotent and at worst accomplices in the strife" (1996, 36). All too often, churches, both their leaders and their congregants, simply echo the biases and bigotry of the empire in which they are embedded. Thus, we should not be surprised if the church of Jesus Christ is dismissed as irrelevant for bringing about change in the world. Nevertheless, the church does have the potential to serve as leaven in our society.

If establishing just relationships is central to the Christian message, then sin can be understood as a breakdown of these relationships, and reconciliation as the process of moving from injustice toward justice, from alienation to communion. For the ministry of reconciliation to be viable for Christians, it must have sacramental roots. The Letter to the Colossians reminds us, "You were once alienated and enemies by your evil deeds. But now [Jesus Christ] has reconciled you, through his physical body and through death, so as to present you holy in his sight without blame and free from accusation" (1:21-22). Theologian Robert J. Schreiter connects the ministry of reconciliation with communion by observing:

> Gathering around the eucharistic table, the broken, damaged, and abused bodies of individual victims and the broken body of the church are taken up into the body of Christ. Christ's body has known torture; it has known shame. In his complete solidarity with victims, he has gone to the limits of violent death. And so his body becomes a holy medicine to heal those broken bodies of today. (1992, 75-76)

The broken body of Christ is not just for my salvation. Surely a highly individualistic reading of the event would miss the more profound implications of the Eucharist. Communion, established "for the forgiveness of sins" (Matt. 26:28), becomes a model for all of us to emulate. Just as God makes room for us who were estranged from God within the divine nature,[3] so too we must make room for others, even those considered enemies. Communion points to the promise of resurrection, the opportunity for life to flow from death, making possible the transformation of enemies into possible companions.

THE PITFALL OF ENDING RACISM AND ETHNIC DISCRIMINATION

Although the church can participate in establishing a ministry of reconciliation, we Christians should not deceive ourselves into believing that eliminating racism and ethnic discrimination will automatically lead to reconciliation. Racism and ethnic discrimination are the symptoms of an unhealthy distribution of power and privilege in this country; they are tied to white supremacy but also extend beyond it. Even if we were to achieve a politically correct social order, injustices would continue to exist unless the present relationships of power and privilege could be radically shifted and altered. The goal should never be to replace one group of oppressors with another group of oppressors that may have a different shade of skin color or different facial features. Reconciliation must always be tied to dismantling the present structures that create power and privilege for some, regardless of who those "some" might be.

THE OPPRESSION OF OPTIMISM

I regularly take groups of students to the less developed parts of the world for immersion experiences. Recently, I planned a trip to a small Christian community in southern Mexico, where we visited and learned from people living in squatter villages and remote indigenous communities. The purpose of these trips is to give a face to the overwhelming global statistics concerning

---

[3] During the Last Supper—the first communion—Jesus prayed that those who were about to break bread and drink the wine of the covenant would become one just as God and Jesus are one (John 17:11).

hunger, disease, and death. In effect, during our stay we commune with, to use a term from Frantz Fanon, "the wretched of the Earth." The poverty we witness is overpowering. The stay in Mexico proved very difficult for a few of the students. Several of them traveled to Mexico with a preconceived notion that they were doing their part for justice. Instead, they were faced with the enormity of neoliberalism's consequences and the futility of any righteous works they might undertake.

At the end of the trip, during our "debriefing" session, some students sought to blame the victims by asking why they have so many babies. Others attempted to seal off guilt and deal with the situation by providing charity. But the majority did have one thing in common. In spite of the misery they witnessed, they still held on to hope and were able to project that hope upon the disenfranchised. But hope can be a final pitfall. Rather than proclaiming hope, I instead shared with the group my deep sense of hopelessness. It is, and continues to be, my belief that regardless of our good intentions, or the praxis we employ, the devastating consequences of global neoliberalism will not only continue throughout my lifetime, but the situation will become even worse as the few get wealthier and the many sink deeper into the despair of stomach-wrenching poverty. The dominant culture, including my liberal students, may be willing to offer charity and to stand in solidarity, but few are willing or able to take a role in dismantling the very global structures designed to privilege them at the expense of others. Liberation is just an illusion unless the privileged status caused by inequalities is rectified. I have slowly come to realize that the reconciliation hoped for will probably not occur in my lifetime, and perhaps not even in the lifetime of my children, or even of my children's children.

As I shared my hopelessness with my fellow travelers I was surprised at their reactions. Some were disturbed. A few grew angry, even to the point of chastising me; in effect, this reaction struck me as an attempt to invalidate my experience and, by extension, the experience of those among the marginalized who also share my concerns. An earnest quest ensued to find "happy" poor people; the students failed to realize that for many of the world's poor and disenfranchised, laughter replaces tears when the tear ducts have dried out from overuse. Afterwards I struggled to understand the cause of their hostile reactions to my expression of hopelessness. A month later I presented an academic paper to fellow scholars on globalization and the forms of possible religiously based praxis that might be employed to counter neoliberalism. In the discussion period that followed, someone commented that I appeared very optimistic about the future. I sincerely apologized if I had given the wrong impression and confessed that if truth be known, I felt quite hopeless about the future. I found it intriguing that the next four scholars from the dominant culture who spoke explained why they felt hope existed and why I should also have hope.

I have often been told that I should end my classes, and my books, with signs of hope. If I fail to do this, students, and readers, may become despondent at the enormity of the situation and simply quit working for justice. Why bother, may become their excuse to do nothing. But, I ask, why must I, as a representative of marginalized communities, provide hope to those with privilege when hope is sorely lacking on the margins? Why, when a person from the margins shares the hopelessness of the situation faced by his or her people, does the dominant culture find it necessary to insist that the oppressed must have hope? Can hope be imposed? Of course, it seems reasonable for those who live in comfortable homes to have hope. Could it be that hope is an ingredient of class privilege? Perhaps, if the disenfranchised dared to share the hopelessness of their situations, those with privilege might realize that their charitable works are simply not sufficient. Is it not then disingenuous to insist that those relegated to the margins of society have this mythical hope even though for generations past, and probably generations to come, they remain trapped by disenfranchisement?

I realize that most studies of issues dealing with reconciliation attempt to end with a word of hope. Instead, I find myself concluding with a confession of hopelessness and failure that I have been unable to see a clear path to reconciliation as I did when I began my careful reading of Jonah. But perhaps, just perhaps, we can be more productive if we don't rely so heavily on hope: the hope of the dominant culture can become a tyranny that prevents action and preserves the elusive nature of reconciliation. When hope becomes an antidote for the guilt of the privileged, eliciting *mea culpa*s and profound apologies, it carries with it a refusal to tamper with self-perpetuating structures that create and reinforce injustice for all of humanity.

So, in the end, what can the privileged members of the dominant culture do? Perhaps there is nothing better than to work at understanding the depth of the situation by spending some time with the disenfranchised in their hopelessness. Accompany us. Sit down with us. Listen quietly to our stories. Job's three friends, Eliphaz of Teman, Bildad of Shuah, and Zophar of Naamath, upon seeing his pitiful situation, tore their garments, threw dust over their heads, and wept aloud. They sat on the ground beside Job for seven days and seven nights, never speaking a word (Job 2:11-12). Sitting in silence and solidarity with Job and his burdens was the best thing they could have done. Note, however, that it is when these friends opened their mouths to guide Job in understanding his situation that they incurred the wrath of God (42:7-9). At that moment, listening was essential. Before the rush to reconcile and move on, it is also essential to grasp the multitude of social structures designed to privilege some with power at the expense of others. Hope becomes a problem if it gets in the way of listening and learning from the oppressed. The semblance of hope becomes an obstacle when it serves a mechanism to maintain rather than challenge the prevailing social structures.

Perhaps if Job's friends would instead have kept silent, listened to Job, and then worked with him in solidarity to restore his dignity, God would have been pleased. Perhaps, if the privileged today share in the hopelessness of the disenfranchised, we may begin to make progress. Such a process can be painful and even frightening, because hopelessness signals a lack of control. Because those who dominate insist always on control, sharing the plight of being vulnerable to forces beyond control might demonstrate clearly how hope can fall short. And perhaps this is the sad paradox—hope can be found only in the hopelessness that was described in Paul's admonition to imitate father Abraham who "beyond all hope believed in hope" (Rom. 4:18).

The familiar text of Qoheleth reminds us that there is a time for every purpose under the heavens: a time to be born and a time to die, a time to kill and a time to heal, a time to mourn and a time to dance, a time to embrace and a time to refrain from embracing, a time to tear and a time to sew together, a time to love and a time to hate, a time for war and a time for peace (Eccl. 3:1-8). Perhaps there is also a time for hopelessness and a time for hope.

Martin Luther King dreamed of a day of reconciliation when "on the red hills of Georgia, the sons of former slaves and the sons of former slave owners will be able to sit down together at the table of brotherhood."[4] But his dream was born only after three hundred years of slavery and an additional hundred years of Jim Crow. For four hundred years, blacks were born into, toiled under, and died in the hopelessness of oppression. Like the children of Israel before them under Egyptian slavery, countless multitudes existed without ever catching a glimpse of liberation, let alone reconciliation. Among Africans and later African Americans, four hundred years of hopelessness never became an excuse for doing nothing. Many worked for liberation, although several failed in the process; others succeeded in planting seeds, individuals such as Nat Turner, Frederick Douglass, Sojourner Truth, Harriet Tubman, Fannie Lou Hamer, and W. E. B. Du Bois, to name a few. The seeds they planted in the hopelessness of their times found fruit in individuals like Martin Luther King Jr. as well as Malcolm X and Rosa Parks.

The hope offered by the dominant culture appears to me to be too contrived, too forced. Such temporal hope holds little sway in the world of the exploited. To be blunt, I hold little if any hope for reconciliation in my time. Nevertheless, any glimmer of hope that might exist must lie in the eschatological, or future, nature of reconciliation. Theologian Juan Luis Segundo insists that reconciliation is one and the same time, both past (something already given through Christ) and future (because of this recon-

---

[4] It is important to note that Cherokees, Muskogees, Uchis, and other Native peoples were driven off the "red hills of Georgia" so that slaveholders could create cotton plantations. Are the "sons of former" native landholders also invited to "sit down together at the table of brotherhood"? And if so, when do they become part of the equation for reconciliation?

ciliation, we will be saved). Reconciliation for Segundo is "already, but not yet" (1993, 39-40). Work for justice, liberation, and reconciliation is not undertaken because the hope of success exists. The disenfranchised must undertake this work because there is no other alternative. For the majority of the world's disenfranchised who find no justice during their lifetime, hope may exist in the eschatological promise of God, beyond our time and our space, for full salvation. And hope possibly exists in that the seeds of justice planted today as a result of the Christ-event will bear fruit in some future generation. But even in the absence of any assurance of future success, the work toward reconciliation must continue for its own sake. This is what it means to be a Christian, to view reconciliation with all of God's creation with eternal eyes.

Poor Jonah. He lacked eternal eyes. He sat on that hill overlooking Nineveh expecting God to smite his enemies. Instead, God spared them from divine wrath. We can only speculate on the outcome if Jonah had preached a message of justice instead of a message of impending doom. In the end, however, the full conversion of the Ninevites failed to occur and within a generation Israel lay in ruins. Maybe this outcome would have been unchanged, yet, in the hopelessness in which the marginalized found themselves, perhaps reconciliation might have prevented some of the misery and death for the victims of empire. Jonah's failure was refusing "beyond all hope [to] believe in hope." Today, we may have somewhat better opportunities than Jonah in bringing the empire to repentance, a repentance rooted in radical social change. I am convinced that those of us from marginalized communities are called to be prophets, like Jonah, to today's beneficiaries of empire, carrying the gift of salvation and liberation. The primary spiritual gift that marginalized communities can offer the privileged of the empire is the discovery of their souls and their humanity, if only they will not bury their heads in hope, but rather seek justice during their quest for reconciliation.

6

Case Studies

What Would Jonah Do?

THE TEACHING OF ETHICS by Euroamericans—what has come
to be thought of as normative—is based on the teaching of ethical theory. Even when case studies are used, the purpose of a case
study is not so much to determine what to do in a particular situation, but rather what ethical principles to employ. Objectivity
is essential in reaching a decision or providing a response, and it
is assumed that any subjectivity that might influence the theoriz-
ing process will be eliminated. This is why case studies are usually based on hypothetical rather than real situations, although
real situations may be modified to create the case.

Using case studies in this manner, however, usually creates a
false dichotomy between ethical theory and practice and can
undo the purpose of using a case study in the first place. Indeed,
to be relevant, case studies must be contextualized in the lived
experience of people, and for our purposes here, in the lived experience of people and communities of color. This final chapter will
explore several case studies unapologetically anchored in the
experience of society's disenfranchised communities. By ground-
ing case studies in the everyday, we can wrestle with how best to
bring about justice and, hopefully, reconciliation. We have
already discussed how Jonah would approach such case studies,
and now our task is to discover how we would approach them.

Below you will not find fictional case studies that will promote
debate of so-called objective and abstract theories, but rather case

studies rooted in the actual responses of disenfranchised communities to injustices with the hope of seeking reconciliation. After reading through each case, the task of the reader as an individual or as a member of a group is to discuss the questions at the end in order to contextualize the difficulty of working for reconciliation. The questions are not designed to determine what ethical philosophy should be employed, but rather to understand the reality in which marginalized groups are forced to exist and what actions should be contemplated that might move communities closer to a justice-based society. The reader is expected to answer these questions by using the somewhat fluid model developed throughout this book.

In the book's introduction (p. 8), I reintroduced the "hermeneutical circle" that appeared in my earlier work, *Doing Christian Ethics from the Margins*. This hermeneutical circle, I maintain, can be an effective model when considering how to bring about reconciliation, liberation, and salvation from the margins. In fact, the circle is the foundation on which I have structured this book. After re-reading the story of Jonah in the first chapter, the second chapter, "Who Was Jonah? What Was Nineveh?" attempted to demonstrate how the first step of the hermeneutical circle—observing by means of an epistemological and historical analysis—is accomplished. The second step of reflecting through socio-scientific analysis was followed in the third chapter, titled "Reflecting on Jonah." The third step of the hermeneutical circle, praying by engaging in a theological and biblical analysis, was demonstrated in the fourth chapter of this book, "Praying through Jonah." While the fourth step, which consists of acting by implementing praxis, is left to the reader to undertake, nevertheless, the final step of the circle, reassessing in order to consider possible new ethical perspectives, was explored in the fifth chapter, "Pitfalls Jonah Should Avoid." Now it is the reader's turn to implement this model.

As the following case studies are read, the reader should attempt to follow the steps of the hermeneutical circle. It can be helpful if the reader answers the questions from the perspective of the marginalized community involved. If the reader is a member of such a community, this task may be easier. If not, I encourage the reader to resist the temptation to try to justify the positions of the dominant culture. Instead, the reader should try to read, think, and decide on possible courses of action *as if* she or he were among the marginalized.

Case Study 1:
Protesting the Columbus Day Parade

In 1907, Colorado was the first state in the Union to establish a Columbus Day holiday. Within two years, others states, specifically New York and Pennsylvania, followed suit. However it was not until 1971 that Columbus Day became a national holiday. One of the ways Columbus Day has traditionally been celebrated in Colorado is with a parade, a practice in which people eventually lost interest and which then ceased to occur. By 1989, however, in preparation for the upcoming quincentennial in 1992 of Columbus's historic voyage, civic leaders in Denver decided to reintroduce the parade. It is not surprising that Native Americans found the idea of a parade celebrating Columbus to be highly offensive.

That Columbus sadistically massacred Native Americans is well documented. Native Americans who refused to submit to Columbus's rule would have their noses cut off. In other instances, indigenous people were castrated and forced to eat their own dirt-encrusted testicles. Or they were simply thrown to the dogs. Bartolomé de Las Casas, an eyewitness to these atrocities in Latin America, wrote that the Spanish soldiers would test the sharpness of their swords and the strength of their muscles by placing bets on their ability to slice off heads or cut bodies in half with just one blow. While living in what would become Cuba, he recorded the deaths of seven thousand children within a three-month period because their overworked mothers were so famished they were unable to produce any milk to nurse them. In short, Columbus's entry into what was to be called the West Indies caused women to be raped, children to be disemboweled, and men to fall prey to the invaders' swords. Within a generation, the Taínos, the indigenous people who discovered the lost

Columbus off their shores, came close to extinction (De La Torre 2002b, 3, 15).

Is it any surprise that Native people are offended that a parade exists that celebrates an individual who murdered and enslaved their people and stole their land? It might be akin to wondering why Jews would be upset with a Hitler Day parade. But the offense is not limited to Native peoples. Over eighty different organizations joined the American Indian Movement (AIM) in their attempts to stop the Denver Columbus Day parade. Leaders of the coalition held endless meetings with parade organizers but with no success. In 1990, they organized a protest march to take place along the parade route. By 1992, they succeeded in stopping the parade for good—until 2000 when the parade was resurrected by another group. Again, leaders of AIM approached the parade organizers to voice their concerns, but they were rebuffed. Failing to get parade organizers to reconsider, AIM, along with other non-Indian organizations, protested the parade. They were able on three occasions to interrupt the parade, although many protestors were arrested.

I interviewed one of the protest organizers, Tink Tinker. He said, "We tried to go through the political channels, but the deck is stacked against us. The only way that we can get the attention of the political establishment is through direct action, including civil disobedience." Since 1989, the American Indian Movement has been calling upon Denver's mayors to take a moral stand against the Columbus Day parade. In fact, AIM members promised in 2005 to cease their protests against the Columbus Day parade if the mayor and city council of Denver honored their request to denounce the parade and review how U.S. history is taught. Their request was ignored.

Questions to Consider

1. It has been 415 years since Columbus arrived in the Western Hemisphere and for the first 121 years since the establishment of the Republic, Columbus Day was not celebrated. Is Columbus Day a federal holiday or an ethnic holiday? What global role did the United States assume in the world in 1907 that would make a

Columbus Day celebration advantageous? What does a Columbus Day celebration have to do with empire building?

2. In 2005 I attended the Columbus Day parade. Arriving ten minutes before the parade started, I found it strange that there were no people in the dozen barricaded streets. After walking several blocks along the parade route, I found an intersection with about two dozen individuals waving Italian flags. Within minutes, several hundred protestors joined them. Apart from the protestors, the next largest group present was the Denver police force. If not for the protestors and police in attendance, there would have been more people marching in the parade than watching it.

Considering the cost to Denver taxpayers for such a massive police presence, one must ask, why hold the parade? Who benefits? What symbol is being preserved? AIM organizers have said that if the parade is renamed the Italian Heritage Parade, they will march with the Italians.

Why does Denver persist in honoring a figure who is so offensive to Native peoples? Should Native peoples continue to protest the parade? If they stopped protesting, would anyone attend? What is the purpose of their continuing protest?

3. On October 2, 2006, parade organizers flew in a Comanche Indian from Oklahoma and held a news conference. David Yeagley, who holds a Ph.D. in music composition, told the media that he did not consider "Columbus to be a threat to American Indians. [But rather] consider[ed Colorado University professor] Ward Churchill to be more threatening to American Indians." He went on to explain that "Columbus was not responsible for the 500 years of history" that followed his sailing from Spain to the Caribbean. Although some claim Columbus was responsible for the "genocide" of American Indians that followed, Yeagley insists that "Columbus never made it to the [U.S.] mainland and never met an American Indian." Three representatives of the American Indian Movement, who were not invited to the news conference but attended anyway, challenged Yeagley as an extreme right-wing conservative whose writings have attacked the Rev. Martin Luther King Jr. and the notion that "innocents" are being killed in Iraq. One of the representatives, Glenn Spagnuolo, an Italian-

American affiliated with AIM, said, "You wrote once that Martin Luther King Jr. was a 'blight' on American history and that women and children in Iraq should be destroyed so that they don't grow up to be terrorists."[1]

Yeagley's comments and presence raised some interesting questions. Who can speak for any one group? In this situation, could Yeagley? Could the representatives of AIM? How are spokespersons from marginalized groups determined? What characteristics and/or experiences should a person possess to be identified with a marginalized group?

Yeagley went on to state that he "want[s] Indians who protest Columbus to re-evaluate the effect of long-term resettlements. I want them to weigh the psychological damage that negative thinking has on young people, how it stifles their natural ambitions, their intuitive aspirations. I want Indians instead to lead in American patriotism and to recover the true role in American society of host, guide and savior."

How do Native peoples, given their history, become American patriots? Do protesting and civil disobedience cause "psychological damage" to indigenous young people?

CASE STUDY 2:
BEFRIENDING THE KU KLUX KLAN

Daryl Davis is a black man who has experienced racism all his life. As a Cub Scout he was pelted with rocks and bottles when marching in a parade. When he was a young teenager, a speaker at his high school pointed him out to announce that his hope was to ship Davis, and all other blacks, back to Africa. As an adult he was beaten and arrested for driving under the influence of being black. These life experiences led him to search for the core reason why some people hated him simply because of the color of his skin, and he began to seek out members of the Ku Klux Klan to interview them about their worldview. He ended up befriending

---

[1] Mike McPhee, "Protest Vowed for Columbus Day Fete: Continuing Enmity Between Members of AIM and Some Italian-Americans Is on Display at a News Conference," *Denver Post*, October 3, 2006.

several of them. This, of course, was a long process. Davis's approach was simply to converse with Klan members and politely but firmly challenge the logic they employed to justify their hatred. If they turned to the Bible to justify their actions, Davis would pull out a Bible and ask them to point to the passage in question. When they made stereotypical remarks, Davis debunked the logic of those remarks. He conducted interviews with some of the leading figures in the Klan, several of whom were later incarcerated for their roles in attempting murder. Through the process, many Klan members got to know and respect Davis as a person rather than a caricature, a knowledge that led some to renounce the Klan.

Davis's goal was not to expunge the Klan's history of violence and terror, but rather to introduce himself to those who hated him because he was black. He wanted to know why the Klan considered him the enemy. Throughout his journey, Davis never offered forgiveness in the name of African Americans, nor in his own name. He simply participated in a journey of the mind, heart, and spirit, attempting to understand hatred, specifically hatred toward him by people who didn't know him personally.

Questions to Consider

1. Several in the black community questioned Davis's methodology. Davis, a church deacon who considers himself a Christian and a believer in Jesus Christ, defended his actions by reminiscing about his grandfather, who was once approached at a train station by Klansmen who threatened to lynch him unless he was on the next train out of town. His grandfather replied that if they let him go, he would run and catch the train that just left. Sitting and having a civil conversation with the Grand Dragon of the United Klans of America, Davis wondered what his grandfather would think if he could see such a sight. He concludes that "knowing my grandfather believed there was good in all people, I somehow know he would have approved."

Davis is no apologist for the views of the Klan, nor does he condone blacks who wish to respond to the Klan with violence. He believes that "the healing power of God is so great, a person, organization or even a nation can be reborn" (Davis 1998, 72, 79, 260). What role does the concept of the *imago Dei* play in Davis's thinking? Can the Klan be redeemed? Is it realistic to think that the Klan can be reborn? Many Klan members interviewed by Davis still hold to their racist worldviews, although a few have been converted. If Davis's approach to the Klan is to be rejected, what then should be the Christian's response?

2. Because of his friendship with Klan members, Davis has collected an array of Klan robes given to him by those who left the organization. Still, some criticize his actions, even suggesting that he is a "sellout." Davis responds by stating,

> I have Klan robes, given to me voluntarily, hanging in my closet. Klansmembers have invited me to their homes for dinner. And some members have quit the Klan as a result of getting to know and respect me and my non-racist beliefs. Time and exposure is a great healer—perhaps the only healer for irrational fear and hatred. Laws can be made to take people out of the Klan, but laws cannot be made to take the Klan mentality out of people. The best way we can learn to respect each other is to know each other. (Davis 1998, 309)

Is Davis correct? Have his actions led some to repentance, making reconciliation possible? Or is the project too individualistic, leading to reconciliation among individuals rather than groups? If Davis waits for the Klan to seek reconciliation first, how long will he have to wait? By taking action, is Davis breaking the cycle of waiting for the dominant culture to establish the framework for reconciliation?

3. Chester Doles was the Imperial Wizard of the Territorial Klans of America, a self-proclaimed white supremacist who predicted a coming race war where one's uniform would be the color of one's skin. Davis began a relationship with Doles that was interrupted when Doles was imprisoned after being charged with "assault with intent to murder." Jailed, with his bail set at $750,000, Doles left behind a nineteen-year-old girlfriend who was eight months pregnant. Davis committed to visiting him in

jail regularly. Furthermore, he gave money to Doles's girlfriend, realizing that she would need help making ends meet with her boyfriend incarcerated and the upcoming birth of her child. This led Doles to confess that Davis has "shown me that [he is] more of a friend when I'm in a jam than half the Klan." Davis justifies his actions by concluding that "whether or not Chester Doles ever changes his feelings towards members of another religion or race, one thing is for sure; he is a Klansman who will never forget and can never deny that a Black man helped keep food on his children's table" (1998, 232, 250-51).

Jesus said that we are to love our enemies and pray for those who persecute us (Matt. 5:44). Is this what Davis is doing? What does it mean to love one's enemy? What does it mean to hold one's enemies accountable for their acts of injustice? How would you show love for your enemies? Are Davis's actions toward the Klan an example of what individual (as opposed to communal) forgiveness looks like?

CASE STUDY 3:
RAISING CONSCIOUSNESS THROUGH THE ARTS

Holland, Michigan, a lakeside town known for its Dutch heritage and tulips, became the site in 2001 for a new Latino art and film festival known as Tulipanes (the Spanish word for tulips). According to the festival's founder, Deborah De La Torre,[2] "There are a lot of first-, second-, and third-generation Hispanics and/or Latinos/Latinas who have lost touch with aspects of their culture. This is one way for them to reconnect with the artistic part." Not only was the festival geared to "celebrate the cultural and artistic heritage of Spanish-speaking people, [but also] their contributions to the local economy and community."[3] The founder also committed to make all the events free to the public, so that everyone, regardless of ability to pay, could attend. Not

---

[2] Deborah De La Torre is my wife; I served on the festival's board of directors for several years.

[3] Shandra Martinez, "Film Festival to Celebrate Latino Culture, Artistic Heritage," *Grand Rapids Press*, February 25, 2001.

only was the consciousness of area Hispanics raised, but so was the consciousness of their Euroamerican neighbors, as regional awareness of Hispanic art forms had been generally limited to folk dancing and mariachi music. In spite of operating with a relatively small budget for such a large-scale endeavor, the festival's big vision brought to Holland, Michigan, classical performers, documentary and feature films, nationally acclaimed scholars, world-renowned works of art, and internationally recognized celebrities.

The success of the festival was partly due to assembling a board of directors comprised of Hispanics and Euroamerican community leaders. Several of the Euroamerican board members were not necessarily versed in Latina/o culture, but were eager to learn and advance diversity for the sake of the community. And while their involvement with the festival was motivated by a desire to make the city more multicultural, their participation inevitably provided a window through which they could witness some of the harsh realities of being a Hispanic in Holland.

On one occasion, the festival needed access to some government documents to determine if a particular site could be used as an office. When the Latina founder of the festival contacted the city official to learn the process, she was told to go to the library and look it up. When this was reported to the board of directors, one of the members, a respected Euroamerican businessman, said he would take care of it. Calling the same official, he received a very different response. The official not only copied the requested documents, but hand-delivered them. Afterward, I asked this businessman why he had received a different response than when a Latina called. He thought for a while and responded that it must have been because he wasn't Hispanic. Because he chose to accompany Latino/as in their quest to raise consciousness, he saw firsthand what Hispanics face on a daily basis. He developed a deeper appreciation for the Latina/o struggle to survive and became a major ally in sharing with his fellow Euroamerican business leaders the importance of hiring and treating the Hispanic community with dignity.

This is but one example. As Hispanics and Euroamericans worked together throughout the year on the festival's planning,

Euroamericans began to hear stories of the difficulties Hispanics faced in getting bank loans, opening checking accounts, finding housing in white neighborhoods, or helping their children get into college. They also heard that many Hispanics in the neighborhood were arriving late to work because they were being pulled over by the police to check their papers. Many of these business leaders, seeing and hearing of these experiences for the first time, took a new approach toward the Hispanic community.

Questions to Consider

1. The purpose of Tulipanes was to raise consciousness among the Hispanic community. In the process, it also raised consciousness among the city's Euroamerican business leaders. Because of Tulipanes, some Hispanics found increased opportunities to dialogue productively with influential members of the dominant social structures. What other types of ventures can leaders of the dominant culture and members of marginalized community work on together? How important is it for the leadership in such collaborative projects to remain in the hands of the marginalized group? What would happen if Euroamericans ran a Latino festival? How do Euroamericans become allies of marginalized groups? What role can allies play in raising consciousness? Do they lead or follow?

2. At one point, Euroamerican members of the board of directors called a local site to to see if it would be possible to host the festival's yearly gala. The site owners refused to make the location available because they were concerned that the attendees of a Hispanic gala would "get drunk and fall down." The board members making the inquiry were angered by the response, particularly when they had previously secured this same location for other private events they had sponsored. It took a while for them to realize that Hispanics were being stereotyped, and now, by association, they too would receive similar treatment. To accompany the marginalized at times means rejection by one's own group. At times there is a cost for Euroamericans to work with disenfranchised groups for justice.

If you are a Euroamerican, what price are you willing to pay to stand in solidarity with a marginalized community that, due to history, may never fully trust you? What does it mean to accompany the marginalized—to share their struggles and their fate? At what point do you choose not to stay in the struggle, to simply walk away?

3. In a letter to the editors of the local newspaper, one of the city's residents blasted city sponsorship of the festival, because Tulipanes's schedule of films that year included the documentary *School of Assassins*, which explored the responsibility of the School of the Americas (now renamed the Western Hemisphere Institute for Security Cooperation) for training right-wing military juntas of Latin America in counter-insurgency techniques, procedures documented to include torture. The letter's author went on to state, "It is simply wrong for them to ask for taxpayer dollars to promote a 'culture' and then use them to promote their narrow, personal political agenda by showing such films as *School of Assassins*. It was not only bad taste; it was also poor judgment."[4] The festival organizers chose this particular film to show the link between U.S. foreign policies and the causes of immigration to this country. Discussions were held after the film to explore such connections.

Is there a connection between art and politics? How can art provide a means of raising consciousness by exposing causes of marginalization? If so, should art be used to raise political issues concerning oppression? Do Euroamericans have a right to dictate what is and what is not acceptable Latina/o art? Do governmental agencies providing grants have a right to stipulate what films are appropriate in cultural festivals?

CASE STUDY 4:
LIVING WITH THE MARGINALIZED

In 1983, the community of northwest Pasadena had the highest daytime crime rate in southern California. The corner at Navarro Avenue and Howard was known by the dubious title of

---

[4] Thomas Volkema, "Tulipanes Had Political Agenda," *The Holland Sentinel*, October 20, 2001.

"blood corner." It was here that most drive-by shootings and failed drug deals in the area occurred. It is also here that the Harambee Center opened its doors. The center's founders, Drs. John and Vera Mae Perkins, dreamed of establishing racial and economic reconciliation. Themselves victims of repeated harassment due to their race, they attempted to create a community based on the reconciliation of whites and blacks, only to later change its focus to reconciliation between Latinos/as and blacks. The Perkinses believed that the only legitimate way to become agents of change in this community was to become a part of it, and so they moved into the neighborhood. The Center opened within two hundred yards of at least forty known drug dealers. Since then, Harambee has served a twelve-block area, working specifically with African American and Latino children and families.

Harambee is the Swahili word for "Let's Push Together." The Center's present leadership is made up of a multiethnic staff led by Rudy and Kafi Carrasco. The Center's mission is to provide a safe place where children and youth can learn and develop into indigenous leaders for northwest Pasadena and beyond. They believe that the most creative long-term solutions to the problems faced by the marginalized must be developed through grassroots and church-based efforts. They feel that only those who see themselves as replacements, or as agents, of Jesus here on earth can bring about positive change within their neighborhoods and communities.

The Center was established on eight essential principles known as "Christian Community Development." The first three are based on the "Three R's" developed by John Perkins (Perkins 1995, 21-22). The rest were developed during a forty-year process by many Christians attempting to answer the question, What response will Christians provide to the troubles of the poor and the inner cities today? Then working together among the poor, rather than in the classroom, the remaining five essential principles were developed. The eight principles are these:

1. Relocation—one must live with the oppressed.
2. Reconciliation (evangelism)—between people and God, and among people.

3. Redistribution (a just distribution of resources)—if God's people who have resources live with the poor, then their skills and resources can be applied to the problems of their community.
4. Leadership development—with the goal not of developing programs but of developing people from an early age.
5. Listening to communities—rather than relying on outsiders to "fix" the problem of the poor, it is those living within the community that work toward their own liberation.
6. Church-based—it is in the church where racial, economic, and educational barriers must first be dismantled.
7. Holistic approach—simplistic answers to complex community dysfunctionalities are rejected; no single answer exists, therefore, different approaches are employed.
8. Empowerment—by creating opportunities by which people can meet their own needs, and those of their neighbors.[5]

Questions to Consider

1. Harambee sees reconciliation coming about not through programs but through a commitment to live together. When the poor, specifically those of color, move into middle-class neighborhoods, "white flight"—whites selling their homes and moving out before prices drop—occurs. Even among the poor, success is defined by the ability to move out of a poor neighborhood to an affluent suburb. Harambee challenges this paradigm by asking those with resources to move into poor neighborhoods. Harambee bases its commitment to solidarity on the Gospel of John, which tells us that the "Word became flesh and dwelt among us" (John 1:14). Jesus relocated, refusing to live in heaven and commute to earth to work in his ministry. Only by living with the disenfranchised is consciousness raised for the person relocating, so that she or he can better understand the real problems facing the marginalized and begin to look for real solutions. A personal stake in the development of the community is thus established.

Living with the oppressed becomes an incarnational ministry.

---

[5] See http://www.ccda.org/?p=9.

How practical is this? Is this what is meant by "solidarity" or "accompaniment"? If not, then how are these terms to be defined? Can one live in middle- or upper-class comfort and effectively minister to the marginalized? Can an "outsider" ever become an "insider"?

2. The Harambee model stresses that justice is available only to those with the economic means to acquire it. When poor neighborhoods are abandoned by those with economic privilege, justice leaves with them, leaving in its wake unjust housing and hiring practices, along with unjust educational and judicial systems.

Is justice indeed a privilege obtained through economic means? Is salvation possible for poor communities only with an influx of the middle and upper economic classes? How will such a move change a neighborhood? Would gentrification set in, raising the cost of home ownership as the neighborhood changes and becomes more desirable, especially if it is located close to the center of town? How does one safeguard against squeezing out those one hopes to be in solidarity with by moving into the neighborhood?

3. There are over six hundred organizations in over two hundred cities and forty states that have implemented the Harambee model and are practicing Christian community development. The following poem best summarizes their philosophy:

> Live among them,
> Learn from them,
> Love them,
> Start with what they know,
> Build on what they have:
> But of the best leaders
> When their task is done,
> The people will remark,
> "We have done it ourselves."

No doubt success stories of this model can be repeated. People's lives have radically changed for the better, with many likely saved from the violence of living in marginalized communities.

Still, the wealthy continue to enrich themselves at the expense of the poorest segments of society, as the income gap reaches new levels. In spite of the success of such programs, how do we deal with the expansion of empire and its impact on the marginalized? How does the continuing inequitable redistribution of wealth upward work against the efforts of such communities? These communities have a local or regional focus. How would a global focus impact their actions? Is such a focus even necessary?

CASE STUDY 5:
A U.S. TRUTH AND RECONCILIATION COMMISSION

On the morning of November 3, 1979, a march was planned to protest unjust working conditions in the Greensboro textile industry. Protestors, blacks and whites alike, mainly from the poorest communities of Greensboro, gathered at Carver and Everett Street around 10 o'clock in the morning at the starting point of the march. Organizers hoped to show how the establishment (including the Klan) used racism to divide and frighten people who have a common link through poverty. Around 11:23 a caravan of cars full of Klan and Nazi members, with a cache of weapons in their trunks, arrived at the march's starting point. Racial slurs were shouted from the cars and some of the marchers responded by shouting back and kicking the slowly passing vehicles. Someone fired a shot from the front of the caravan. As protestors rushed away from where the shot took place, toward the rear of the caravan, Klan and Nazi members poured out and began attacking the protestors. Quickly they went back to their cars, only to return with firearms, shooting at marchers and killing several of them.[6]

On June 12, 2004, for the first time in the history of the United States, a Truth and Reconciliation commission was set up to examine "the context, causes, sequence and consequence of the

---

[6] Accounts of the events are based on the testimony given by Rev. Nelson N. Johnson, an organizer of the march, to the Greensboro Truth and Reconciliation Commission. He was present during these events and suffered minor injuries after being stabbed by a Nazi.

events of November 3, 1979" for the purpose of bringing healing and transformation to a community scared by those events. The specific goals of the commission were (1) the healing and reconciliation of the community, (2) clarification of the confusion caused by these events and their aftermath, (3) providing a means to acknowledge and recognize the feelings of those involved, and (4) helping to facilitate positive changes in social consciousness and community institutions. The final product of the commission's work was a report of its findings, which included specific recommendations for the Greensboro community and its institutions on how to make greater strides toward concrete healing, reconciliation, and restorative justice.

Questions to Consider

1. City officials and community leaders have repeatedly said that the events of November 1979 had nothing to do with race. Did they? Why or why not? This appeared to be an attack by avowed hate groups in the middle of an African American neighborhood that was ignited by racial slurs rooted in a history of white supremacy. Was this what it was?

Many Klan and Nazi members involved were also poor and struggling to survive financially. How is racism used to the benefit of wealthy white community leaders? Could a common struggle for living wages be used to bring about reconciliation between poor whites and people of color who are also poor? Why would corporate leaders oppose such a reconciliation? The owners of the local textile mills, politicians, and government officials may not necessarily belong to the Klan or Nazi Party, but can they manipulate such groups to their benefit? If so, how? Why was the Klan's message about the march framed as an effort of blacks wanting to dominate whites?

What benefits does whiteness provide to Klan and Nazi members, even if they are poor? What benefits exist for those in power when they scapegoat the actions of hate groups? What benefits exist for average white Americans who also scapegoat the actions of hate groups?

2. Police knew, from a paid informant, that the Klan, the Nazis, and members of the Rights of White People were planning to confront demonstrators at the march. Yet they provided no protection to the marchers, nor did they warn them of the impending danger. The media spun the story as a confrontation between the Klan and communists and in this way turned the event into an ideological squabble—a planned shoot-out between the two groups.

On November 17, 1980, an all-white jury acquitted the Klan and Nazi members, even though several videos showed specific Klan and Nazi members firing guns. Additionally, none of those involved in the events, or the families of victims, were allowed to testify. On April 15, 1984, a federal trial also acquitted the defendants.

What do you do when the police, government officials, the media, and the court system fail to protect your human rights? What alternative exists when the political structures prevent justice from being carried out? What alternatives exist after you follow all the rules to address injustices, but the rules are stacked against you?

3. Truth and Reconciliation commissions are based on the assumption that successful transitions from conflict and resentment to peace and unity cannot occur unless the past is confronted and reckoned with. Can a community ever reconcile if it refuses to deal with its past? Is a Truth and Reconciliation commission dealing with a history of racism and racial discrimination a way of dealing with this U.S. use of violence in the past to protect and secure the privilege of the few? Can Truth and Reconciliation commissions be used as cosmetics, to scapegoat a particular group of individuals rather than deal with the root causes of injustices? If those privileged by society are not forced to attend, then what can a Truth and Reconciliation commission accomplish? Can a Truth and Reconciliation commission and its findings simply be ignored by the dominant culture? Can there ever be racial and ethnic reconciliation in the United States apart from a Truth and Reconciliation commission?

Bibliography

Alumkal, Antony W. 2004. "American Evangelicalism in the Post-Civil Rights Era: A Racial Formation Theory Analysis." *Sociology of Religion* 65, no. 3:195-213.

Anderson, Sarah, John Cavanagh, Chris Hartman, and Betsy Leondar-Wright. 2001. *Executive Excess 2001: Layoffs–Tax rebates–the Gender Gap.* Washington, D.C.: Institute for Policy Studies and United for a Fair Economy.

Aulén, Gustaf. 1969. *Christus Victor: An Historical Study of the Three Main Types of the Idea of the Atonement.* Translated by A. G. Hebert. New York: Macmillan.

Battle, Michael. 2000. "The Ubuntu Theology of Desmond Tutu." *Interpretation* 54, no. 2:172-82.

Bash, Anthony, and Melanie Bash. 2004. "Early Christian Thinking." In *Forgiveness in Context: Theology and Psychology in Creative Dialogue,* edited by Fraser Watts and Liz Gulliford. London: T&T Clark International.

Bhabha, Homi K. 1994. *The Location of Culture.* New York: Routledge.

Bickerman, E. J. 1965. "Les deux erreurs du prophète Jonas." *Revue de l'Histoire et de Philosophie Religieuses* 45:232-64.

Biggar, Nigel. 2003. "Making Peace or Doing Justice." In *Burying the Past: Making Peace and Doing Justice after Civil Conflict,* edited by Nigel Biggar. Washington, D.C.: Georgetown University Press.

Boff, Leonardo. 1978. *Jesus Christ Liberator: A Critical Christology for Our Times.* Translated by Patrick Hughes. Maryknoll, N.Y.: Orbis Books.

Bolin, Thomas M. 1997. *Freedom beyond Forgiveness: The Book of Jonah Re-Examined.* Sheffield: Sheffield Academic Press.

Bonhoeffer, Dietrich. 1963. *The Cost of Discipleship.* Translated by R. H. Fuller and Irmgard Booth. New York: Macmillan.

Bork, Robert H. 1996. *Slouching towards Gomorrah: Modern Liberalism and the American Decline.* New York: Regan Books.

Broshi, Magen. 1974. "The Expansion of Jerusalem in the Reigns of Hezekiah and Menasseh." *Israel Exploration Journal* 24:21-26.

Cannon, Katie G., and Carter Heyward. 1994. "Can We Be Different but Not Alienated? An Exchange of Letters." In *Feminist Theological Ethics: A Reader.* Louisville: Westminster John Knox.

Chapman, Audrey R. 2001. "Truth Commissions as Instruments of Forgiveness and Reconciliation." In *Forgiveness and Reconciliation: Religion, Public Policy & Conflict Transformation*, edited by Raymond G. Helmick, S.J., and Rodney L. Petersen. Philadelphia: Templeton Foundation Press.

Chomsky, Noam. 2003. *Hegemony or Survival: America's Quest for Global Dominance*. New York: Henry Holt.

Clingan, Ralph Garlin. 2002. *Against Cheap Grace in a World Come of Age: A Study in the Hermeneutics of Adam Clayton Powell, 1865-1953, in His Intellectual Context*. New York: Peter Lang.

Coleman, Paul. 1998. "The Process of Forgiveness in Marriage and the Family." In *Exploring Forgiveness*, edited by Robert D. Enright and Joanna North. Madison: University of Wisconsin Press.

Columbus, Christopher. 1960. *The Journal of Christopher Columbus*. Translated by Cecil Jane. New York: Clarkson N. Potter.

Comblin, José. 1986. "O tema de reconciliação e a teologia na America Latina." *Revista Eclesiástica Brasileira* 46, no. 182:272-314.

Cone, James H. 1975. *God of the Oppressed*. San Francisco: Harper & Row.

Cooper, Mary H. 1998. "Income Inequality." *Congressional Quarterly Researcher* 8, no. 15 (April 17):339-59.

Davis, Daryl. 1998. *Klan-Destine Relationships: A Black Man's Odyssey in the Ku Klux Klan*. Far Hills, N.H.: New Horizon Press.

Daye, Russell. 2004. *Political Forgiveness: Lessons from South Africa*. Maryknoll, N.Y.: Orbis Books.

De Gruchy, John W. 2002. *Reconciliation: Restoring Justice*. Minneapolis: Fortress.

De La Torre, Miguel A. 2002a. *Reading the Bible from the Margins*. Maryknoll, N.Y.: Orbis Books.

———. 2002b. *The Quest for the Cuban Christ: A Historical Search*. Gainesville: University Press of Florida.

———. 2003. La Lucha *for Cuba: Religion and Politics on the Streets of Miami*. Berkeley: University of California Press.

———. 2004. *Doing Christian Ethics from the Margins*. Maryknoll, N.Y.: Orbis Books.

Enright, Robert, and Richard Fitzgibbons. 2000. *Helping Clients Forgive: An Empirical Guide for Resolving Anger and Restoring Hope*. Washington D.C.: American Psychological Association.

Fanon, Frantz. 1963. *The Wretched of the Earth*. Translated by Constance Farrington. New York: Grove Press.

Foucault, Michel. 1980. *Power/Knowledge: Selected Interviews and Other Writings 1972-1977*. Edited and translated by Colin Gordon. New York: Pantheon Books.

————. 1984. *The Foucault Reader*. Edited by Paul Rabinow. New York: Pantheon Books.

Frank, Andre Gunder. 1969. *Capitalism and Underdevelopment in Latin America: Historical Studies of Chile and Brazil*. Middlesex: Penguin Books.

Freire, Paulo. 1994. *Pedagogy of the Oppressed*. New York: Continuum International.

Fromm, Erich. 1951. *The Forgotten Language: An Introduction to the Understanding of Dreams, Fairy Tales and Myths*. New York: Rinehart.

Gandhi, Mahatma. 2004. *The Essential Writings of Mahatma Gandhi*. Edited by Raghavan Iyer. New York: Oxford University Press.

Girard, René. 1986. *The Scapegoat*. Translated by Yvonne Freccero. Baltimore: Johns Hopkins University Press.

————. 1987. *Things Hidden since the Foundation of the World*. Translated by Stephen Bann and Michael Metteer. London: Athlone.

Golka, Friedemann W. 1988. "Jonah." In *Revelation of God: A Commentary on the Books of The Song of Songs and Jonah*, edited by Fredrick Carlson Holmgren and George A. F. Knight. Grand Rapids: Eerdmans.

Goodspeed, George Stephen. 1902. *A History of the Babylonians and Assyrians*. New York: Charles Scribner's Sons.

Gramsci, Antonio. 1971. *Selections from the Prison Notebook*. Edited by Quinton Hoare and Geoffrey Nowell-Smith. New York: International Publishers.

Grayson, A. K. 1991. "Assyrian Civilization." In *The Cambridge Ancient History*, 2nd ed., vol. 3, pt. 2, *The Assyrian and Babylonian Empires and Other States of the Near East, from the Eight to the Sixth Centuries B.C.*, edited by John Boardman et al. Cambridge: Cambridge University Press.

Gulliford, Liz. 2004. "Intrapersonal Forgiveness." In *Forgiveness in Context: Theology and Psychology in Creative Dialogue*, edited by Fraser Watts and Liz Gulliford. London: T&T Clark International.

Gutiérrez, Gustavo. 1988. *A Theology of Liberation: History, Politics, and Salvation*. Rev. ed. Translated by Sister Caridad Inda and John Eagleson. Maryknoll, N.Y.: Orbis Books.

Hamber, Brandon. 2003. "Does the Truth Heal? A Psychological Perspective on Political Strategies for Dealing with the Legacy of Political Violence." In *Burying the Past: Making Peace and Doing Justice after Civil Conflict*, edited by Nigel Biggar. Washington, D.C.: Georgetown Press.

Hardt, Michael, and Antonio Negri. 2001. *Empire*. Cambridge, Mass.: Harvard University Press.

Hopkins, Dwight N. 2000. *Shoes That Fit Our Feet: Sources for a Constructive Black Theology*. Maryknoll, N.Y.: Orbis Books.

Hoyt, Thomas. 1991. "Interpreting Biblical Scholarship for the Black Church Tradition." In *Stony the Road We Trod: African American Biblical Interpretation*, edited by Cain Hope Felder. Minneapolis: Fortress.

Kee, Alistair. 2005. "The Criticism of [Black] Theology Is Transformed into the Criticism of Politics." In *The Quest for Liberation and Reconciliation: Essays in Honor of J. Deotis Roberts*, edited by Michael Battle. Louisville: Westminster John Knox.

Kennedy, Paul. 1987. *The Rise and Fall of the Great Powers: Economic Change and Military Conflict from 1500 to 2000*. New York: Random House.

Kidwell, Clara Sue, Homer Noley, and George E. "Tink" Tinker. 2001. *A Native American Theology*. Maryknoll, N.Y.: Orbis Books.

King, Martin Luther. 1963. *Strength to Love*. Philadelphia: Fortress.

Kissinger, Henry A. 1974. *American Foreign Policy*. New York: W. W. Norton.

Lacan, Jacques. 1977. *Écrits: A Selection*. Translated by Alan Sheridan. New York: W. W. Norton.

Lacocque, André, and Pierre-Emmanuel Lacocque. 1981. *The Jonah Complex*. Atlanta: John Knox Press.

Læssøe, Jørgen. 1963. *People of Ancient Assyria: Their Inscriptions and Correspondence*. Translated by F. S. Leigh-Browne. London: Routledge & Kegan Paul.

Landes, George M. 1967. "The 'Three Days and Three Nights' Motif in Jonah 2:1." *Journal of Biblical Literature* 86:446-50.

Lederach, John Paul. 1997. *Building Peace: Sustainable Reconciliation in Divided Societies*. Washington D.C.: U.S. Institute of Peace.

Levinson, Nan. 2003. *Outspoken: Free Speech Stories*. Berkeley: University of California Press.

Madhloum, Tariq. 1967. "Excavations at Nineveh." *Sumer* 23:76-82.

Madison, James. 1961. "No. 10." In *The Federalist Papers*, edited by Alexander Hamilton, James Madison, and John Jay. New York: New American Library.

Nietzche, Friedrich. 1956. *The Genealogy of Morals*. Translated by Francis Golffing. New York: Doubleday.

———. 1966. *Beyond Good and Evil: Prelude to a Philosophy of the Future*. Translated by Walter Kaufmann. New York: Vintage Books.

Olmstead, A. T. 1951. *History of Assyria*. Chicago: University of Chicago Press.

O'Sullivan, John. 1845. "Annexation." *United States Magazine and Democratic Review* 17, no. 1 (July and August):5-10.

Parrot, André. 1955. *Nineveh and the Old Testament*. London: SCM.

Pearce, Jenny. 1982. *Under the Eagle: U.S. Intervention in Central America and the Caribbean*. Cambridge, Mass.: South End.

Perkins, John. 1995. *Resurrecting Hope: Powerful Stories on How God Is Moving to Reach Our Cities*. Ventura, Calif.: Regal Books.

Phillips, Kevin. 1990. *The Politics of Rich and Poor: Wealth and the American Electorate in the Reagan Aftermath*. New York: Random House.

Roberts, J. Deotis. 1994. *Liberation and Reconciliation*. Maryknoll, N.Y.: Orbis Books.

Said, Edward. 1993. *Culture and Imperialism*. New York: Alfred A. Knopf.

Santayana, George. 1936. *Life of Reason or The Phases of Human Progress*, vol. 1. New York: Charles Scribner's Sons.

Sasson, Jack M. 1990. *Jonah: A New Translation with Introduction, Commentary, and Interpretation*. Anchor Bible 24B. New York: Doubleday.

Scherman, Rabbi Nosson, and Rabbi Meir Zlotowitz. 1978. *The Twelve Prophets: Jonah—A New Translation with a Commentary Anthologized from Talmudic, Midrashic and Rabbinic Sources*. Brooklyn, N.Y.: Mesorah.

Schreiter, Robert J. 1992. *Reconciliation: Mission & Ministry in a Changing Social Order*. Maryknoll, N.Y.: Orbis Books.

———. 1998. *The Ministry of Reconciliation: Spirituality & Strategies*. Maryknoll, N.Y.: Orbis Books.

Scott, James C. 1990. *Domination and the Arts of Resistance: Hidden Transcripts*. New Haven: Yale University Press.

Segundo, Juan Luis. 1993. *Signs of the Times: Theological Reflections*. Translated by Robert R. Barr. Maryknoll, N.Y.: Orbis Books.

Shriver, Donald W. 2001. "A Bridge across Abysses of Revenge." In *Forgiveness and Reconciliation: Religion, Public Policy, & Conflict Transformation*, edited by Raymond G. Helmick, S.J., and Rodney L. Petersen. Philadelphia: Templeton Foundation Press.

Simon, Uriel. 1999. *The JPS Bible Commentary: Jonah*. Philadelphia: Jewish Publication Society.

Simons, J. 1959. *The Geographical and Topographical Texts of the Old Testament*. Leiden: E. J. Brill.

Smith, Robert F. 1963. *What Happened in Cuba? A Documentary History*. New York: Twayne.

Sugirtharajah, R. S. 2001. *The Bible and the Third World: Precolonial, Colonial and Postcolonial Encounters*. Cambridge: Cambridge University Press.

Takaki, Ronald. 1993. *A Different Mirror: A History of Multicultural America*. Boston: Little, Brown.

Taylor, Mark Kline. 1990. *Remembering Esperanza: A Cultural-Political Theology for North American Praxis*. Maryknoll, N.Y.: Orbis Books.

Thandeka. 1999. *Learning to Be White: Money, Race, and God in America*. New York: Continuum.

Thornton, Sharon G. 2002. *Broken Yet Beloved: A Pastoral Theology of the Cross*. St. Louis: Chalice.

Tillich, Paul. 1969. *What Is Religion?* Edited by James Luther Adams. New York: Harper & Row.

Tinker, George E. (Tink). 2004. "American Indian Traditions." In *Handbook of U.S. Theologies of Liberation*, edited by Miguel A. De La Torre. St. Louis: Chalice.

Volf, Miroslav. 1996. *Exclusion & Embrace: A Theological Exploration of Identity, Otherness, and Reconciliation*. Nashville: Abingdon.

Walker, Alice. 1984. *In Search of Our Mothers' Gardens: Womanist Prose*. London: Women's Press.

West, Cornel. 2004. *Democracy Matters: Winning the Fight Against Imperialism*. New York: Penguin Books.

Williams, Delores S. 1993. *Sisters in the Wilderness: The Challenge of Womanist God-Talk*. Maryknoll, N.Y.: Orbis Books.

Williams, Eric. 1944. *Capitalism & Slavery*. Chapel Hill: University of North Carolina Press.

Wilson, William Julius. 1999. *The Bridge over the Racial Divide: Rising Inequality and Coalition Politics*. Berkeley: University of California Press.

Winant, Howard. 2004. *The New Politics of Race: Globalism, Difference, Justice*. Minneapolis: University of Minnesota Press.

Wolff, Hans Walter. 1977. *Obadiah and Jonah: A Commentary*. Minneapolis: Augsburg.

Zinn, Howard. 2003. *A People's History of the United States: 1492-Present*. New York: Perennial Classics.

Zlotowitz, Meir. 1980. *Yonah/Jonah: A New Translation with a Commentary Anthologized from Midrashic and Rabbinic Sources*. Brooklyn, N.Y.: Mesorah.

Index